SHARKS

DISCOVER THEIR UNDERWATER WORLD!

This edition published by Parragon Inc. in 2016

Parragon Inc.
440 Park Avenue South, 13th Floor
New York, NY 10016
www.parragon.com

Copyright © Parragon Books Ltd 2013–2016

Edited by Grace Harvey and Philip de Ste. Croix
Designed by Francesca Winterman and Sue Pressley
Cover design by Kathryn Davies
Consultant: Philip de Ste. Croix
Designed, produced, and packaged by Stonecastle Graphics Ltd

ISBN 978-1-4748-3192-5

Printed in China

Discovery KIDS™

SHARKS

DISCOVER THEIR UNDERWATER WORLD!

PaRragon

Bath • New York • Cologne • Melbourne • Delhi
Hong Kong • Shenzhen • Singapore • Amsterdam

CONTENTS

INTRODUCTION

Sharks are found in all the oceans of the world.
Some are fierce meat-eaters that rip their prey
to shreds, others feed on tiny plants and animals,
called plankton, that drift along in the ocean currents.

Our planet was formed around 4.5 billion years
ago. The first living creatures appeared roughly
1.2 billion years later. Life in the oceans evolved
slowly, until sharks appeared around 400 million
years ago. Since then, sharks have evolved into
over 470 different species.

The longest existing modern sharks are the
cow sharks (sixgill and sevengill), which date
back 190 million years. These primitive species
can be found in the deep sea. The newest
modern sharks are the hammerheads, which
are thought to date back 50 million years.
Sharks are among the oldest creatures that have
been living continuously on Earth.

The term *shark* was first used in 1569 to
advertise a specimen that was brought back
to London, England, and exhibited there.
Sailors had caught it during an expedition to
South America commanded by the famous
Elizabethan seaman Captain John Hawkins.
Why the sailors called this fish a "shark" remains
a mystery.

Sharks live in various marine habitats around
the world. Most prefer temperate and tropical
waters, but some are found in colder seas near
the North and South Poles. They range from
the shallow waters near the coastline right out
to the open ocean, and some even live in deep
waters where light does not reach.

WHAT IS A SHARK?

Sharks are fish that live in the seas and oceans all over the world. There are over 470 different species of shark. They have been living on Earth for 400 million years. The shape of a shark is so perfectly adapted to living in the water that it hasn't changed much in all that time.

DIFFERENT TYPES OF SHARK

Some sharks are tiny, others are giants. Some are gentle, and some are fierce. Some swim very fast to catch their prey in the open sea. Others move slowly and feed on animals that live on the ocean floor.

Fin
Stiff fins are supported by rods of cartilage.

Gills
Gills are used to breathe.

Snout
The snout is often sharply pointed. The mouth is shaped like a crescent.

DISCOVERY FACT™

Inside most fish is an air-filled swim bladder, which keeps the fish afloat. Sharks don't have swim bladders. Instead, they have oil-filled livers that help them float. Most, however, have to keep swimming or they sink.

Dogfish have long, slim bodies to slip through the water.

Wobbegongs hide on the seabed. They are well camouflaged.

Tail
A strong pointed tail fin pushes the shark through the water.

Angel sharks have flat bodies. They also hide on the seabed.

Basking sharks live in open water. They are often seen swimming very close to the coastline.

AMAZING SHARKS

Can you imagine a fish that has a head shaped like a hammer? Or one that can gobble up a sea lion whole? Sharks are some of the world's most amazing creatures.

Great white shark

The great white shark eats other sharks for dinner—along with whole penguins, seals, and sea lions.

Whale shark

The gentle whale shark is the world's biggest fish. It weighs as much as two elephants and can grow longer than a bus.

Mako shark

The bullet-shaped mako shark can swim at over 43 miles per hour. It is one of the fastest fish in the ocean.

Hammerhead shark

The hammerhead shark has eyes on each side of its head. It swings its head from side to side to get an all-around view.

DISCOVERY FACT™

Sharks don't have bones. Their skeletons are made from light, stretchy cartilage. This is the same kind of material that humans have in their ears and noses.

Hammerhead sharks have smaller pectoral fins than other species of shark.

TEETH

Teeth are a shark's most important weapon. They are designed to help it catch and eat prey.

Sharks have multiple rows of teeth. Every time a shark loses a tooth, the tooth in the row behind it moves forward to take the lost tooth's place.

The shape of a shark's tooth depends on its diet. Sharks that eat fish have long, narrow teeth for gripping slippery fish. Sharks that eat mammals such as seal, have sharp, jagged teeth for ripping flesh. Sharks that eat shellfish have thick, platelike teeth to crush the shells of their prey.

Sharks' teeth are not rooted in the jaw like ours, but are attached to the skin covering the jaw.

Unlike most animals' jaws, both the shark's upper and lower jaws move. It bites with its lower jaw first and then its upper.

The great white shark has sharp, pointy teeth, perfect for ripping flesh.

The prehistoric shark Megalodon may have been up to 65 feet long. Here is one of its huge teeth next to the tooth of a modern shark.

The powerful tail of a great white shark helps propel it through the water, to attack prey.

The small cookiecutter shark swims up to a larger fish, takes a bite out of its side (the shape of a cookie), and swims away again very quickly!

HOW SHARKS SWIM

Most sharks are graceful and powerful swimmers. Their smooth bodies are perfect for moving underwater. Sharks swim in S-shaped movements, powered by their tails.

Dorsal fin
The stiff fin on a shark's back hel▮ with balance.

Tail

The shark's tail is a little bit like its motor. It sweeps it from side to side in long strokes, powering its body forward. The streamlined shape of the shark's body helps it glide through the water. Sharks with large tails can accelerate very quickly.

Pectoral fins
Fins on each side of a shark's body help it stee▮

Fins

The dorsal fin on the shark's back acts like the keel of a boat. It stops the shark from rolling over in the water. The pectoral fins on the sides help to move the shark up and down in the water, like the wings of an aircraft.

DISCOVERY FACT™

Sharks cannot swim backward. This is because a shark's stiff pectoral fins cannot bend upward (unlike those of most other fish), so they are unable to back up.

Tail

A shark's long tail beats from side to side, pushing the shark forward through the water.

Types of tail

The caudal, or tail, fins of sharks vary a lot in shape and size. The top half of the fin is usually larger than the bottom half because the shark's backbone extends into the upper half of the fin.

Tiger shark

Nurse shark

Porbeagle

Thresher shark

Great white shark

Cookiecutter shark

Slow motion

Whale sharks are slow swimmers, cruising along at about 3 miles per hour. They swim by moving their entire bodies from side to side, not just their tails.

Thresher shark

The thresher shark has the longest tail of any shark—its upper part is almost as long as the rest of the shark's body. When hunting fish, thresher sharks are known to "slap" the water with their tail to stun their prey before eating it.

SENSES AND HUNTING

Sharks are always seeking out their next meal. They can see, hear, touch, and smell, just like people. But their senses are much more powerful than ours and are perfectly adapted to working in water.

Touch

Finding food
A shark uses all its senses to find prey, but smell gives it some of the most important clues. A shark can smell a tiny amount of blood in the water from hundreds of feet away.

Touch
A lateral line along their sides helps sharks pick up movements in the water around them.

Hearing
A shark's ears can hear sounds traveling through the water. The ears lie beneath small holes in the shark's head.

Extra sense

Sharks have special jelly-filled receptors in their heads. These extra sense organs let sharks pick up the faint electric signals given off by fish. This sense is particularly powerful in hammerhead sharks.

Sight

Hearing

Smell

Sight

A shark's eyes can see well in dim underwater light.

Smell

A shark does not breathe through its nose. It is just used for detecting smell.

MOTHERS AND PUPS

All baby sharks are born from eggs and are known as pups. The eggs of most sharks grow inside their mother. A few kinds of shark lay their eggs on the seabed, safe inside tough egg cases.

All sharks are born from eggs that are fertilized by sperm from the male shark. But the eggs can grow in different ways. In some sharks, they remain inside the mother's body and hatch inside her. The young shark pups are then born as live fish, ready to swim away.

Other sharks lay their eggs inside tough, leathery egg cases in the water. The pup grows inside the egg case feeding on the yolk inside it. When it is ready to be born, the young shark wriggles its way out of the case, which splits open.

Little hammerheads

Baby hammerhead sharks are born with their heads bent backward, so they don't get stuck inside their mother.

Egg cases

Dogfish eggs are protected by an egg case called a mermaid's purse. The babies grow inside, feeding on the egg yolk.

A blue shark mother can give birth to 50 or more babies at a time. The record for this shark is 135 pups. They take 9 to 12 months to grow big enough to be born.

Groups of sharks

Sharks do not remain in a family group. When sharks are seen together in a large group, it is usually because a lot of food is available to be eaten.

Lemon sharks

Lemon shark eggs grow inside their mother. She gives birth to tiny pups, which soon swim off to find food. They remain in fairly shallow water while they grow to their adult size of almost 7 feet long. This can take between 12 and 15 years.

THE SHARK'S WORLD

Our Earth is often called the blue planet because more than two-thirds of its surface is covered by water. Most of this water is found in the oceans. This is where the sharks have their home. They live in shallow waters around the world's coasts and in deeper water all the way down to the ocean floor.

THE OCEANS

There are five oceans. The largest is the Pacific Ocean, which stretches between North and South America, Australia, and the eastern coast of Asia. The smallest is the Arctic Ocean, which surrounds the North Pole. All five of the world's oceans are connected. Smaller areas of water, called seas, are joined to some of the oceans. These include the Caribbean, Mediterranean, and North Seas.

Greenland

ARCTIC OCEAN

North Sea

ATLANTIC OCEAN

Europe

Asia

North America

Mediterranean Sea

PACIFIC OCEAN

Caribbean Sea

Africa

PACIFIC OCEAN

South America

ATLANTIC OCEAN

INDIAN OCEAN

Australia

SOUTHERN OCEAN

Ocean islands

Oceans are mostly wide, open areas of water. Islands are scattered across the oceans. These pieces of land rise up from under the water. Islands may cover large areas of land or just a few square miles.

A small island in the Indian Ocean.

Coral reefs

Coral reefs are found off coasts and around islands in tropical parts of the world. Reefs are home to many kinds of fish, including reef sharks, and other colorful marine animals.

Coral reefs are built from the skeletons of tiny sea animals.

DISCOVERY FACT™

Sharks play an important role in keeping our oceans healthy. Most sharks are at the top of the food chain, and they eat old or sick marine animals. The animals that survive are the fittest ones.

SHARKS IN ANCIENT TIMES

Humans have been exploring the world by sea for thousands of years. Sharks have always been a danger to people whose work takes them out onto or into the ocean. Nearly 2000 years ago, the ancient Roman author Pliny wrote about sharks attacking men who were diving for sponges.

Hawaiian myth

Sharks have been both feared and worshiped by human beings since ancient times. In Hawaiian myth, a shark god created the universe and everything in it.

Ancient bond

Humans have collected sharks' teeth for thousands of years. People used to believe they would give some of the unique predatory abilities of sharks.

DISCOVERY FACT™

When the dinosaurs' cousins, the plesiosaurs, went extinct, prehistoric sharks became the main predators in the oceans. They have evolved into the sharks we know today.

WAVES

Waves are created by wind blowing over the surface of the water. The stronger the wind, the bigger the waves. Waves travel across the ocean, just like ripples cross a pond. When waves reach shallow water near a coast, they slow down and become taller. Finally, the top, or crest, of the wave topples over and crashes down onto the shore.

Tsunamis

Tsunamis are waves created by earthquakes under the water. By the time the waves reach the coast, they may be many feet tall. Powerful tsunamis can cause a lot of damage.

In 2004, ships destroyed by a tsunami in Thailand landed over half a mile from the coast.

DISCOVERY FACT™

Sharks have been seen riding inside big waves, coming to shore like surfers do.

Surfing

Riding a surfboard on the crest of a wave is an exciting sport. Skilled surfers can twist and turn, jump in the air, and ride their boards right under the wave as it rises up and curls over. A lot of shark attacks happen when a shark takes a bite out of a surfer or his or her board.

TIDES

Twice a day, the sea rises up on a shore and then falls back again. High tide is when the sea reaches its highest point on a shore, and low tide is when it is at its lowest point on the shore.

Low tide

At low tide, the sea exposes the entire shore. In some places, the difference between high and low tides is great, but in others, it is very small.

The Sun and the Moon

The tides are caused by the pull of the Sun and the Moon. This pull is called gravity, and it pulls the Earth's oceans toward the Sun and Moon. This creates a bulge of water that produces the high tides. At the same time, there is less water in other parts of the ocean, and this is what causes the low tides.

Sun

Moon's orbit

Sun's pull on the Earth

Less water at low tides

Bulge of water produces high tides

Moon

Moon's pull on the Earth

DISCOVERY FACT™

The largest tide in the world occurs in the Bay of Fundy in Canada. Here, the sea level changes by a massive 53 feet.

Sharks at low tide

Sharks can get trapped by the tides. They sometimes get stuck in lagoons and small bays during low tides. They are unable to get back to the open sea. People swimming in lagoons at low tide need to keep an eye open for sharks.

BULL SHARK

The bull shark is a fierce predator that will eat almost anything that it comes across. It is solitary, usually choosing to hunt by itself.

The bull shark is large and has a wide body in relation to its length. It is colored gray on top and off-white below.

It is one of the few sharks that can live in freshwater. Bull sharks are often seen in rivers and lakes. One was even spotted 2,480 miles upstream in the Amazon River in Iquitos, Peru.

Bull sharks eat all kinds of animals in the water, and this includes other sharks, especially the sandbar shark. They sometimes use a "bump and bite" technique, headbutting their victim first before biting it.

Bull sharks are one of the most dangerous sharks to humans because they are aggressive and often come into shallow coastal waters where people swim and surf. Many of the recorded attacks on people have been made by bull sharks.

Snout
This is wider than it is long, which is unusual for a shark.

Body
The bull shark has a much wider body in relation to its length than most other sharks

Profile

Length:	Average 7 ft (males), 11.5 ft (females)
Weight:	Average 200 lb (males), 287 lb (females)
Order:	Ground sharks
Family:	Requiem sharks
Diet:	Fish (including other sharks), dolphins, turtles, birds, invertebrates

Location

Bull sharks are found worldwide in the coastal waters of tropical and subtropical (more than 64 °F) seas and sometimes in rivers. They swim from the surface to about 100 feet deep.

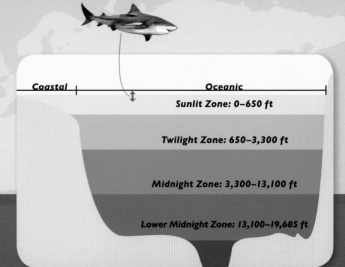

Coastal | Oceanic

Sunlit Zone: 0–650 ft

Twilight Zone: 650–3,300 ft

Midnight Zone: 3,300–13,100 ft

Lower Midnight Zone: 13,100–19,685 ft

OCEAN CURRENTS

Oceans are never still. Flows of water in the oceans, called currents, travel around the world. Currents of warm water flow from the equator toward the poles. Cold currents start in the Arctic and Antarctic and flow toward the equator.

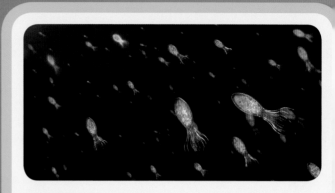

Plankton

Sometimes, an ocean current brings up lots of food from the seabed. Tiny plants and animals, called plankton, feed well and increase in number, forming a plankton bloom. A plankton bloom can change the color of the water and measure several hundred miles across.

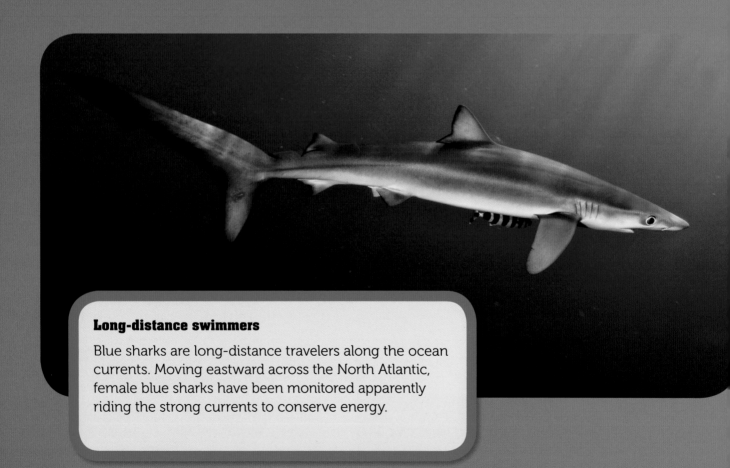

Long-distance swimmers

Blue sharks are long-distance travelers along the ocean currents. Moving eastward across the North Atlantic, female blue sharks have been monitored apparently riding the strong currents to conserve energy.

Arctic Ocean

Greenland

Arctic Ocean

NORTH
AMERICA

EUROPE

ASIA

Atlantic
Ocean

Pacific Ocean

AFRICA

SOUTH
AMERICA

Indian Ocean

AUSTRALIA

Pacific Ocean

Southern Ocean

Warm current   Cold current

DISCOVERY FACT™

The Gulf Stream is an
ocean current that flows
across the Atlantic Ocean
from the Caribbean Sea to
western Europe. It measures
about 50–93 miles wide.

Lots of fish

Some ocean currents
are high in nutrients and
encourage plankton to
grow. This attracts fish
that feed on the plankton.
The large numbers of fish
attract predators such
as seabirds.

OCEAN WEATHER

Oceans play an important role in the world's weather. Tropical storms, hurricanes, and waterspouts all form over water.

Storm clouds gather over the Caribbean Sea.

Tropical storms

Rain falls most days in the regions nearest the equator, called the tropics. Storm clouds form off the coast during the day and bring a heavy downpour of rain at night.

DISCOVERY FACT™

It seems that sharks are able to sense the approach of storms. Different species of shark have been spotted swimming toward deeper water in the Caribbean Sea as a hurricane was moving their way.

The eye of the hurricane

Hurricanes

Hurricanes are huge, spinning storms that form over warm water. Strong hurricane winds with speeds of up to 200 miles per hour can cause a lot of damage if they move onto land.

Waterspout

A waterspout is a spinning column of air and water that moves over water. It looks just like a miniature tornado. Although a waterspout is not as dangerous as a tornado, it can damage small boats.

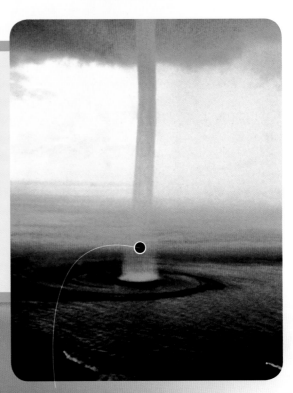

A waterspout viewed from an aircraft.

Monsoon

Each year, winds from the Indian Ocean bring heavy rain to Southeast Asia. These winds are called monsoons, and they last several months. The monsoon season ends when the winds change direction and blow away from land.

Monsoon rains falling in India.

Bull shark

Bull sharks swim close to shore and in freshwater rivers and lakes. For this reason, they are likely to encounter people swimming and fishing. Its mouth is packed with hundreds of sharp, triangular teeth.

SALT WATER

Seawater tastes very salty. This is because the water contains a lot of dissolved salt. Humans cannot drink seawater because it makes them sick. But animals that live in the sea have ways of coping with the high levels of salt.

Coping with salty water

Sharks can get rid of any excess salt that they ingest. A gland at the end of the intestine absorbs salt from the blood, and it is then excreted.

Adding more salt

Some of the salt in seawater is made when rocks break down, and from hot-water vents on the ocean floor. Volcanic eruptions underwater also add salt to the oceans.

Clouds of steam pour from an undersea volcanic eruption.

Sharks have evolved to live in seawater.

Turtle tears

Turtles have a salt gland behind their eyes. By getting rid of salt through their eyes, nostrils, or tongue, turtles can live in salt water without becoming ill.

Salt pans

When salt water gathers in shallow ponds, the water dries up, leaving behind large areas of salt called salt pans. The salt can be collected and used for cooking.

DISCOVERY FACT™

The water in the Dead Sea in the Middle East is ten times saltier than in the oceans. This is because the sea has no outlets (such as rivers or streams). This means the salt cannot be carried away.

Dry salt is left when the water evaporates.

LIVING IN WATER

Animals that live in water are called aquatic animals. Their bodies are adapted to life in water. Fish have gills to breathe underwater, while seals have flippers to help them swim.

Sharks

Sharks are fish, and they breathe using gills. Water enters through their mouths and passes through the gills, where the oxygen is removed. The oxygen goes into the shark's bloodstream and is pumped around the body by the heart. The water is pumped out of the shark's body through the gill slits back into the sea.

Gills are used to breathe.

DISCOVERY FACT™

Some sharks are not able to pass water through their gills unless they keep swimming forward. This means they cannot rest, but must spend their whole lives swimming in order to breathe.

Crabs

A crab has a heavy outer skeleton covering its body. The crab's body is flat so that it can easily squeeze under and between rocks. Crabs have gills inside their shells and can breathe underwater like fish.

Jellyfish

Jellyfish have a soft body made mostly of water. They must stay in water to keep their shape. If you take a jellyfish out of the water, it will collapse into a blob of jelly (like a gelatin dessert).

Seals

Seals are marine mammals with flippers instead of arms and legs. Although seals live in water, they breathe air and have to return to land to give birth.

Seals have to come up to the surface to breathe air.

FOOD CHAINS

A food chain shows how nutrients pass from plants to animals as one eats the other. In the ocean, plant plankton is eaten by animal plankton, or zooplankton. The zooplankton is eaten by larger animals. These animals are then eaten by even bigger animals. Many sharks have a diet of seals, turtles, fish, and even large seabirds. Some sharks, however, such as the whale shark and basking shark, eat plankton and small fish.

Plant plankton

Plant plankton are at the bottom of the ocean food chains. They are called producers because they make their own food using sunlight.

Top meat-eaters

Top carnivores, or meat-eaters, such as pelicans, sharks, and dolphins, eat fish. A top carnivore is an animal that no other animal eats—they are at the top of the ocean food chain.

Plant-eaters

Zooplankton, or plant-eaters, such as this crab larva, eat the producers, or plant plankton. The plant-eaters are known as primary consumers.

Meat-eaters

Larger animals called the secondary consumers eat the primary consumers. Secondary consumers are hunters. There are many different hunters in the ocean, including fish and squid.

This great white shark has leaped out of the water to catch a seal.

The darker shade of this shark's back blends with the sea, so that it can attack prey from below.

DISCOVERY FACT™

The great white shark attacks its prey from below. It swims until it is only a few yards away, then attacks by turning its head upward and surging up through the water.

BENEATH THE SURFACE

Imagine if you could walk into the sea from a beach. First, you would walk through the shallow water of the continental shelf that extends out from the coast. Then, the seabed slopes down for thousands of feet to the deep ocean floor.

Ocean levels

In some places the continental shelf is narrow, but in others it stretches for hundreds of miles. The continental slope links the continental shelf with the ocean floor, which may be thousands of feet down.

Sea level

Continental shelf

Sea lions

Sea lions swim in the shallow water close to the shore above the continental shelf. They like to pull themselves out of the water and lie on sandy beaches.

Starfish

Starfish are found on the continental shelf. They crawl over the sand hunting for mussels and other shellfish to eat.

The deepest-known part of the ocean is the Mariana Trench in the Pacific Ocean. It lies 6.8 miles below sea level.

Wide-set eyes help the hammerhead shark see above and below at all times.

Hammerhead shark

Sharks, such as this hammerhead shark, are found in both shallow and deep water. Some sharks can dive down several thousand feet to the bottom of the oceans.

Different creatures are found at each depth of the ocean.

Spider crab

Spider crabs are creatures of the seabed. They have been found on the ocean floor more than 10,000 feet below the water's surface.

ontinental
pe

Ocean floor

TIGER SHARK

Tiger sharks get their name from the stripes and spots that cover the bodies of their young. It also reflects their reputation as large and powerful hunters of the seas.

Tiger sharks are gray-brown on top with a light yellow to white underside. These sharks are some of the largest predatory fish in the seas—the biggest can grow up to 18 feet long and weigh more than 1,760 pounds.

Tiger sharks have been called "the garbage cans" of the oceans, since they will eat almost anything. Strange items such as tires, bottles, rolls of chicken wire, and even a crocodile's head have been found in the stomachs of dead tiger sharks.

These sharks are solitary hunters, mostly searching for food at night. They generally swim quite slowly when hunting prey, but they can put in a rapid burst of speed for a vital few seconds when they want to launch an attack.

Teeth
Teeth have sharp, jagged edges that can tear and rip virtually anything—even the shells of turtles.

Profile

Length:	Average 10.5 ft (males), 9.5 ft (females)
Weight:	850–1,400 lb (males and females)
Order:	Ground sharks
Family:	Requiem sharks
Diet:	Fish (including other sharks), turtles, crabs, clams, dolphins, seals, seabirds

Tail fin

The upper part of the tail fin is very long—perfect for swimming quickly as the shark moves in for the kill.

Location

The tiger shark is found worldwide in tropical (more than 64 °F) and some temperate (50–64 °F) waters, from the shoreline to the open sea. They swim from the surface to about 1,115 feet deep.

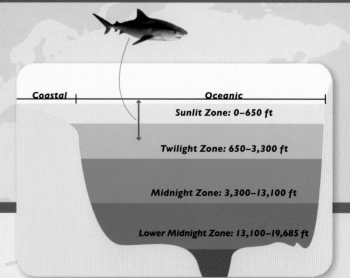

Coastal   Oceanic

Sunlit Zone: 0–650 ft

Twilight Zone: 650–3,300 ft

Midnight Zone: 3,300–13,100 ft

Lower Midnight Zone: 13,100–19,685 ft

DIVING WITH SHARKS

People cannot live in water, but they can dive underwater, using special equipment to help them breathe.

Shark cages allow divers to get very close to large sharks without putting themselves in danger. The sharks are attracted to the cage by the presence of dead fish bait. However, sharks do sometimes show signs of aggression and may attack the cage.

Shark ca•

Discovering wrecks
Shipwrecks in shallow water are popular dive sites. By exploring a wreck, divers can learn a lot about the history of the ship.

Exploring reefs

Many divers like to explore coral reefs. These are good places to find brightly colored fish and other marine creatures, such as dolphins and sea turtles.

DISCOVERY FACT™

Sharks are not normally aggressive around divers. If a shark gets too close to a diver, it is sometimes possible to scare it away just by pushing on its nose, which is very sensitive.

reathing underwater

cuba divers carry a tank of air to elp them breathe underwater. The ank is connected to a regulator, which the diver places in is or her mouth. When he diver breathes in, air ows through the egulator into he mouth.

egulator

Tiger shark

This is one of the largest sharks living today.
It has spots and stripes on its body, particularly
when young. These fade as it gets older. It hunts
mainly at night and will eat almost any large sea
creature that crosses its path.

EXPLORING THE DEEP OCEAN

NORTH AMERICA

The deep ocean is very cold, and the huge pressure would crush a human instantly, but some sharks can be found at depths of more than 11,500 feet. Scientists use hi-tech equipment to explore this part of the ocean.

Underwater features

Using technology, such as submersibles, scientists have made maps of some of the ocean floor. They have found mountain ranges, such as the Mid-Atlantic Ridge, and deep valleys, such as the Mariana Trench in the Pacific Ocean.

This map shows some of the mountain ranges that lie underwater on the ocean bed.

SOUTH AMERIC

Submersibles

Submersibles are specially designed mini submarines that can dive to depths of 36,000 feet. Inside, there is room for only two or three people.

This submersible has a strong frame made from titanium metal up to 2 inches thick.

EUROPE

Atlantic Ocean

The Mid-Atlantic Ridge runs down the middle of the Atlantic Ocean.

AFRICA

DISCOVERY FACT™

The record for the deepest-dwelling shark is held by the Portuguese shark, which has been found at a depth of 12,000 feet. It feeds mainly on fish, octopus, and squid that live near the ocean floor.

ROVs

Remotely operated vehicles (ROVs) are controlled from the surface of the water. These vehicles have mechanical arms to pick up objects and cameras to film any strange creatures.

Deep-sea creatures

Scientists have discovered amazing creatures living deep underwater. They include sea stars, blind shrimplike creatures called amphipods, and comb jellies, which can produce their own light.

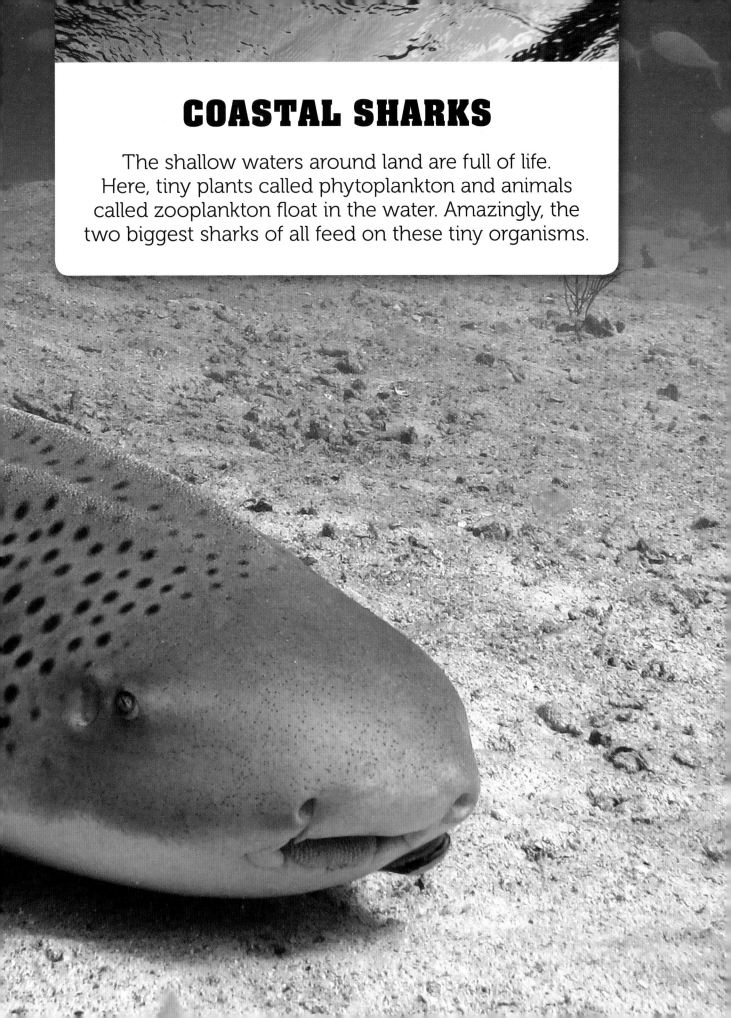

COASTAL SHARKS

The shallow waters around land are full of life. Here, tiny plants called phytoplankton and animals called zooplankton float in the water. Amazingly, the two biggest sharks of all feed on these tiny organisms.

TINY PLANTS

The moving ocean stirs up mud on the seabed. This releases nutrients into the water. These nutrients provide food for tiny plants called phytoplankton that float in the water.

Phytoplankton

Phytoplankton sit at the bottom of the food chain and sharks at the top of it. But the two biggest sharks, the whale shark and the basking shark, feed directly on these tiny organisms. They filter them out of the water with bristly rods called gill rakers.

DISCOVERY FACT™

Just like plants on land, phytoplankton can make their own food using sunlight, carbon dioxide (a gas), and nutrients from the water.

Whale shark

Slow-moving whale sharks scoop up plankton near the surface of the water. These sharks have no teeth. They are called filter feeders.

Diatoms

Diatoms are a type of phytoplankton that have hard, shell-like skeletons. The skeleton is in two parts, called valves, that fit together tightly. There are many types of diatom, each with its own skeleton design.

Plankton bloom

Phytoplankton are able to grow and reproduce very quickly. They can treble in numbers in just one day. Sometimes, there are extra nutrients in the water, and the phytoplankton increase in number. There are so many plankton that the water changes color. This is called a plankton bloom, and it can grow so large it can even be seen from space.

This large plankton bloom off the coast of Argentina.

Dinoflagellates

Dinoflagellates make up much of the phytoplankton. At night, these tiny organisms give out a strange light. This is called bioluminescence.

TINY ANIMALS

The weight of all the plankton in the oceans is greater than that of all the fish, dolphins, and whales put together.

Phytoplankton are eaten by the creatures that make up the animal plankton, or zooplankton. These animals drift in the water, carried around by tides and currents.

Shoals

Fish sometimes hunt for food like plankton in large groups called shoals. These shoals attract larger predators, such as sharks, farther up the food chain.

Microscopic creatures

Most animal plankton is made up of tiny shrimplike creatures called copepods and amphipods. The larvae (young form) of marine animals such as starfish, jellyfish, and barnacles are also called animal plankton.

A blacktip reef shark approaches a large shoal of reef fish on which it can feed.

Jellyfish

Jellyfish are among the largest animal plankton. They have a bell-shaped body and long tentacles that hang below. Many just drift in the water, while others swim by flapping the skirt of their body.

alps

alps are tubelike organisms bout the size of a large eanut. They suck in water nd food at their front nd. The food goes to the omach while the water pumped out at the back. his is what makes the salp ove forward.

Baby fish

Many fish lay their eggs in coastal waters. When they hatch, the baby fish feed on phytoplankton that are floating in the water around them. The small fish grow quickly until they are large enough to swim away from the coast and out to sea.

lps may link together to form ains that are up to 16.5 feet long.

PLANKTON FEEDERS

Animal and plant plankton are the favorite food of many animals, including ocean giants such as the whale shark and basking shark. Most plankton feeders filter, or sieve, tiny organisms from the water.

Basking shark

The basking shark swims along with its mouth wide open. When its mouth is full of water, the fish closes it and squeezes the water out through its gill slits. Any food is trapped inside by rakers (bristle-like filters) in the gills.

Manta ray

Most rays live on the seabed, hunting fish and small animals. The huge manta ray is different. It is an active fish that swims great distances, filtering plankton through its gills.

DISCOVERY FACT™

Scientists believe that some whale sharks may live for up to 180 years. Male whale sharks are not ready to start breeding until they are around 30 years old.

Humpback whales have frilly plates in their mouths that sieve the water.

hale shark

he whale shark is the largest fish in the orld. It usually grows up to 40 feet long nd can weigh more than 22 tons. It is a ter feeder, and despite its size, it is not a angerous shark to humans.

A whale shark's spots are unique and can be used to identify an individual shark, like a human fingerprint.

BASKING SHARK

This incredible-looking shark is the second largest fish (after the whale shark) in the oceans. It may look frightening, but this is a gentle giant. It feeds on tiny plankton as it cruises slowly near the surface.

The body of the basking shark is grayish brown to dark gray, sometimes with lighter patches on the flanks. Its head is quite pointed, but as soon as the shark starts to feed, its appearance changes dramatically. Its huge jaws gape open to allow water to pour over the gill rakers inside its throat. These trap the tiny particles of plankton on which it feeds. This is called filter feeding. More than 343,000 gallons of water—enough to fill two Olympic-sized swimming pools—pass over its bristly gill rakers every hour.

Basking sharks feed near the surface where the tiny plankton organisms are attracted to the sunlight. Fishermen see them fairly often off the coastline. Basking sharks migrate thousands of miles during the winter months, seeking clouds of plankton (called blooms) in warmer waters.

Mouth
A huge mouth like an enormous butterfly net sweeps up tiny food organisms in the water.

Large gill slits
Bristles behind the gill slits, called gill rakers, trap food particles in the water.

Profile

Length:	13–16 ft (males), 24.5–29.5 ft (females)
Weight:	Up to 8,600 lb (males and females)
Order:	Mackerel sharks
Family:	Basking sharks
Diet:	Phytoplankton, zooplankton, tiny fish, fish eggs

Location

The basking shark is found in temperate (50–64 °F) and subpolar (below 50 °F) waters of the North and South Atlantic and Pacific Oceans. They swim from the ocean surface to about 1,870 feet deep.

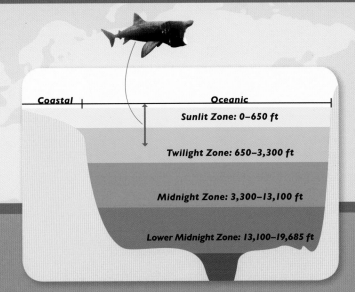

Coastal | Oceanic

Sunlit Zone: 0–650 ft

Twilight Zone: 650–3,300 ft

Midnight Zone: 3,300–13,100 ft

Lower Midnight Zone: 13,100–19,685 ft

KRILL

Krill are among the most important animals in the ocean. There are billions of these small, shrimplike animals. They are eaten by sharks, whales, seals, penguins, and seabirds.

Krill

Living in numbers

Krill live in large groups, called swarms. Up to 30,000 krill can be found in a cubic yard of water. The wriggling swarm confuses hunters.

Squid

Squid catch krill using their long tentacles. Their sharp beaks rip the krill into small pieces for swallowing.

Penguin predator

Krill are an important food for penguins. Chinstrap penguins feed on larger types of krill, while other species of penguin prefer the smaller ones. Penguins, together with whales, seals, and other seabirds, eat about 165–330 million tons of krill each year.

Whale shark

Whale shark feeding

When they come across swarms of krill, whale sharks hurry to get at the food. They lunge at the krill and churn up the surface of the water as they gulp them into their mouths.

DISCOVERY FACT™

Whale sharks are huge, so they have to eat a lot of food to survive. Scientists measured what one young whale shark was eating. It was more than 46 pounds of food every day.

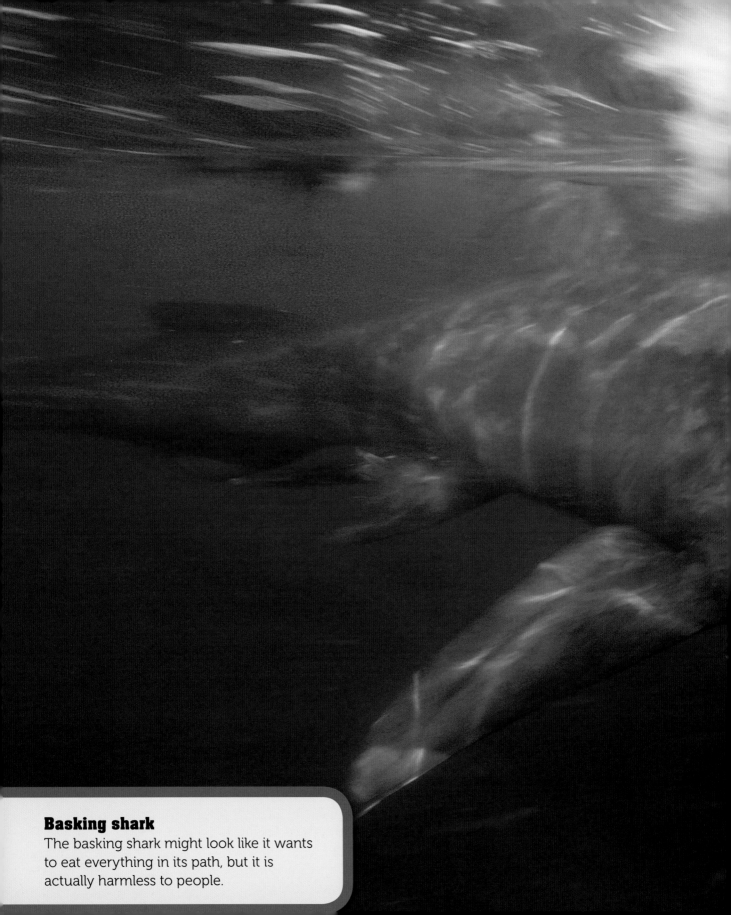

Basking shark
The basking shark might look like it wants to eat everything in its path, but it is actually harmless to people.

SEAWEEDS

Seaweeds are found in shallow waters close to the coast. They are not proper plants because they do not have leaves, stems, or roots, but they do make their own food by photosynthesis. This is when plants take energy from the Sun and create sugars.

Covering rocks

Many seaweeds are found on rocky shores. When they are covered by the tide, their leaflike fronds float in the water. When the tide goes out, they are left piled up on the rocks until the tide returns.

Seaweed washes up on beaches.

Crested horn shark

The crested horn shark is found off the east coast of Australia. The female lays egg cases that are usually attached to fronds of seaweed. The young sharks hatch from the cases after about eight months.

Harvesting seaweed

People harvest seaweed from the sea. It is eaten as a vegetable in Japan and other countries. Seaweeds are also used as an ingredient in skin cream, shampoo, nail polish, ice cream, beer, and paint, and as a fertilizer on soil.

Types of seaweed

There are three main types of seaweed—green, brown, and red. Brown seaweed is the most common and is found on rocky beaches. Green seaweed is found only in very shallow water.

KELP FORESTS

Kelp are large seaweeds that grow closely together. Kelp forests, with their fronds gently moving in the water, are magical places where many animals live.

Thin leaves

Kelp have a stalk with long, thin leaves, called fronds, at the top. They are covered in a protective layer of mucus and feel quite tough, but are easily damaged in storms.

Dense growth

Kelp forests are found in fairly shallow water, where the kelp can get enough sunlight to make food. At the surface, they form a thick, tangled mat.

Leopard sharks

Leopard sharks live in shallow waters and are sometimes seen among the kelp forest, usually staying near the bottom.

DISCOVERY FACT™

There are different types of kelp. The giant kelp is the fastest growing of all. It can increase the length of its fronds by up to 24 inches every day.

A diver explores kelp forests off the coast of California.

Floating plant
A kelp has a balloon-like float at the base of the fronds. The float is full of air. It keeps the fronds floating near the water's surface, where there is more sunlight.

Kelp eater
Sea urchins eat kelp. In some places, there are too many sea urchins. They eat the young kelp before it has a chance to grow—so the forest disappears.

LEOPARD SHARK

Leopard sharks are one of the most common sharks along the coast of California. They live in shallow waters of the bays and estuaries, and they occasionally patrol the kelp forest, usually staying near the bottom.

This handsomely marked shark has silvery-bronze skin that is covered with darker oval spots. These markings are what give it its name. The older a leopard shark is, the paler the spots will be.

Large schools of leopard sharks are a common sight in bays and estuaries. They swim over sandy or muddy flats or rock-strewn areas near kelp beds and reefs. Leopard sharks often follow the tide onto shallow-sloped shorelines to forage for food on the seabed.

Leopard sharks capture their prey by sucking water in with their mouths. This sucks up the food, which is then gripped by the teeth.

Leopard sharks are a target for fishermen, who catch them to sell as food. Live leopard sharks are also sold for keeping in aquariums.

Skin
The silvery-bronze skin is patterned with dark ovals that stretch in a neat row across the back.

Profile

Length:	28–47 in (males), 43–59 in (females)
Weight:	Up to 42 lb maximum (males and females)
Order:	Ground sharks
Family:	Hound sharks
Diet:	Bony fish, crabs, clams, shrimps (right), worms

Mouth
The mouth is on the flat underside of its head, and it opens downward. This is perfect for a shark that skims over the sand to pluck up crabs, clams, and worms.

Location
The leopard shark is found in shallow temperate (50–64 °F) water along the Pacific coast of North America. They swim from the shallows to about 295 feet deep.

Coastal   Oceanic

Sunlit Zone: 0–650 ft

Twilight Zone: 650–3,300 ft

Midnight Zone: 3,300–13,100 ft

Lower Midnight Zone: 13,100–19,685 ft

KELP FOREST ANIMALS

More than 800 types of animal have been found living in kelp forests. There are shoals of brightly colored fish, feeding limpets, lurking blue sharks, and giant rays.

Garibaldi fish

The bright orange garibaldi fish aggressively defends its nest site in the kelp from all—including divers! The male builds a nest in which the female lays her eggs. He then looks after the eggs until they hatch.

Garibaldi fish nest in the kelp forest.

Eagle ray

The eagle ray has huge winglike fins that are up to 6.5 feet wide. It turns on its side to swim between the stalks of the kelp.

Sea otter

Sea otters feed on the sea urchins and clams that they find in the kelp forests. Clams have hard shells, so otters collect stones, which they use to crack open the shells. They balance the stone on their stomach as they hit the clam shell against it.

DISCOVERY FACT™

Sea otters sometimes wrap themselves in kelp. They use it as an anchor so that they do not drift away while they sleep.

Blue shark

The blue shark is a regular visitor to the kelp forest. It hides in the kelp waiting for prey, such as squid, to pass close by.

A blue shark lurking in the kelp forest.

SEAGRASS

There are underwater seagrass meadows along sheltered coasts. The seagrass shelters large numbers of fish and attracts animals such as turtles, manatees, and dolphins. Sharks keep these habitats healthy by intimidating animals that might otherwise overgraze the seagrass.

Underwater grass

Seagrass gets its name from its grasslike appearance, but it is not a proper grass. It is a plant that can grow, rooted in sand, in shallow seawater.

Lobster nursery

Seagrass meadows are nurseries for spiny lobsters. Adult lobsters come here to lay their eggs, out of which hatch baby lobsters. When the lobsters are big enough, they move to nearby swamps and coral reefs.

Manatee

The manatee, or sea cow, looks a bit like a hippopotamus. It has paddle-like front legs to push itself through the water. It uses its large upper lip to graze the seagrass. An adult eats up to 110 pounds of grass every day.

DISCOVERY FACT™

Scientists in Hawaii found that tiger sharks help protect seagrass meadows by frightening away the turtles. When the sharks are not around, turtles may eat so much that the meadow is destroyed.

...rtles graze on ...agrass meadows.

Sandbar shark
This shark is often found swimming over the muddy or sandy bottom of coastal waters in tropical and temperate oceans around the world. It has a very tall fin on its back. Females can grow to more than 6.5 feet in length.

BALEEN WHALES

Like whale sharks, baleen whales are filter feeders. But how they filter feed is completely different. They have comblike plates hanging from the roof of their mouth, called baleen plates, which they use to sieve food from the water.

At more than 100 feet long, the blue whale is the world's largest animal. It is a baleen whale. This giant lives by eating tiny marine organisms and can eat up to 40 million krill a day.

Baleen plates

A whale's baleen plates are made from keratin— the same material your fingernails are made from. The teeth of these plates are known as whalebones.

Whale's baleen plate

Shark attack

Baleen whales are so big that very few animals in the sea can hurt them. But some large sharks will attack and try to eat these huge whales. They target young calves or adult whales that are old or sick, and so unable to defend themselves properly.

Water spray is blown up into the air when whales come up to the surface of the water to breathe.

Blowholes

A blowhole is a whale's nostril, found on top of its head. Whales cannot breathe underwater, so they have to take a deep breath into their lungs before they dive. When they return to the surface, air is forced from their lungs through the blowhole. This sprays water high into the air.

Grooves in this humpback whale's throat allow the throat to expand to four times its usual size when it is feeding.

Breaching

Whales sometimes leap out of the water and fall down with a big splash. This is called breaching. Scientists are unsure why they do this. It may be to signal to other whales, or it may be to remove parasites from their skin.

TOOTHED WHALES

Orcas, pilot whales, dolphins, and porpoises are toothed whales. Toothed whales usually live together in small groups called pods. They are hunters that feed mostly on fish and squid.

Orcas

Orcas (killer whales) are somewhat like sharks and just as dangerous. Some feed only on fish, but most hunt marine mammals, such as sea lions, seals, walruses, and even large whales.

Orcas will surge up onto the beach to catch seals.

Hunting seals

Some orcas living off the coast of South America hav learned how to surf onto beaches to catch seals. The whales have to be careful not to become stranded on the beach.

A killer whale's top and bottom teeth fit together when it shuts its jaws.

Sharp teeth

Most toothed whales have small, cone-shaped teeth, which are perfect for grippi slippery fish. Orcas have about 50 teeth. Dolphins can have up to 100 teeth.

olphin or porpoise?

olphins and porpoises look
ery similar, but a dolphin has
pointed snout and a long,
m body. A porpoise has a
unded fishlike snout and a
orter, rounder body.

A pair of dolphins

DISCOVERY FACT™

Dolphins have
been trained by the
U.S. Navy to scare off large
sharks by butting their gill
pouches. However, they will
not approach a bull shark,
which is known to attack
dolphins in the wild.

NURSE SHARK

The nurse shark is one of the more docile types of shark. It is fairly lazy during the day, resting in groups on the bottom of the sea. It starts moving at night, which is when it hunts for food.

Nurse sharks are yellowish tan to dark brown in color. Young sharks sometimes have small black spots and bands on their skin.

They like warm water and live near the bottom in the shallows, sometimes close to mud or sand flats.

Unlike some sharks, nurse sharks can breathe without having to move through the water. Their respiratory system pumps water over the gills while they rest during the day.

Nurse sharks are bottom feeders. They use their sensitive barbels to search for food in the sand and silt on the ocean floor. They suck up food like a vacuum cleaner, rather than having to grasp it with their teeth.

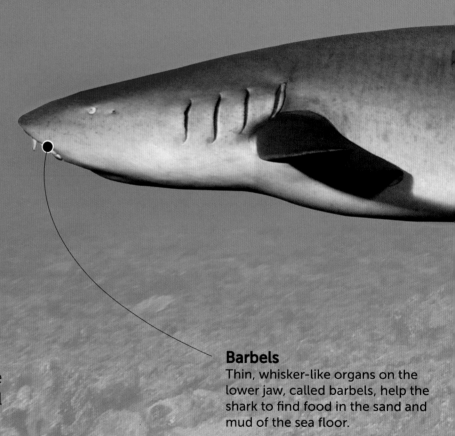

Barbels
Thin, whisker-like organs on the lower jaw, called barbels, help the shark to find food in the sand and mud of the sea floor.

Profile

Length:	Average 6.9 ft (males), average 7.9 ft (females)
Weight:	200–265 lb (males) and 165–231 lb (females)
Order:	Carpet sharks
Family:	Nurse sharks
Diet:	Fish including rays, squid, octopus, crabs, small invertebrates

Tail fin
An extremely long tail fin makes up about a quarter of the shark's length.

Location

Nurse sharks are found in the tropical (more than 64 °F) waters of the western Atlantic and eastern Pacific Oceans. They swim from the shallows to about 230 feet deep.

Coastal	Oceanic
	Sunlit Zone: 0–650 ft
	Twilight Zone: 650–3,300 ft
	Midnight Zone: 3,300–13,100 ft
	Lower Midnight Zone: 13,100–19,685 ft

COASTAL NURSERIES

Many animals visit coastal waters to breed or to have their young. These shallow waters are often sheltered, and there is plenty of food for the young animals.

Hammerhead gathering
Each year, hammerhead sharks gather together in special breeding places. Each male selects a female, and they then mate. After about 10 months, the female swims into shallow water to give birth to her pups.

Hammerhead sharks gather to breed.

DISCOVERY FACT™

The yearly migration of gray whales from Baja California nurseries to the Arctic feeding grounds and back is a distance of about 12,500 miles—the longest journey made by any mammal.

Whale migration

Many whales make regular journeys along the world's coasts. Humpback whales spend the summer in cold waters, where there is plenty of food. They then travel, or migrate, to warmer, shallow water, where the females give birth to their young.

Underwater flier

Manta rays live in the deep sea but give birth in shallow coastal waters, where the young stay for several years. The females are pregnant for about a year before giving birth to one or two pups.

REEF SHARKS

Coral reefs are some of the most colorful places on the planet. They are found in shallow, tropical waters and are home to thousands of different creatures. Several species of reef shark hunt in these waters, preying on fish and other marine animals.

WHERE IN THE WORLD?

Coral reefs are found in warm seas, where the water is shallow and there is plenty of light. Coral will grow only in clean water that is free from pollution.

Reef sharks

Reef sharks are the top predators in their part of the oceans. Scientists know that if reef sharks are healthy and present in good numbers, the health of the reef and the fish that live on it must be good, too.

Reef sharks live in tropical waters and lagoons near coral reefs.

Coral is made of polyps. These are tiny animals with tentacles, a little like sea anemones

Great Barrier Reef

The Great Barrier Reef is the world's largest coral reef. It runs along the northeast coast of Australia and is 1,550 miles long. Almost 6,000 different species of animal live on this reef.

DISCOVERY FACT™

The Great Barrier Reef is the largest structure made by living creatures on Earth. It is so large that it can even be seen from space.

Reefs around the world

Most coral reefs are found in the Indian and Pacific Oceans, the Caribbean, and the Red Sea. Corals are not found where there are cold ocean currents or where large rivers flow into the sea.

Greenland

Arctic Ocean

ASIA

EUROPE

NORTH
AMERICA

Atlantic
Ocean

Pacific
Ocean

AFRICA

Pacific Ocean

SOUTH
AMERICA

Indian
Ocean

AUSTRALIA

Southern Ocean

☐ Coral reefs

LIVING REEF

Coral reefs are built by hard corals. These are coral animals that leave behind a stony skeleton when they die. Their skeletons create a habitat in which other animals can live.

Coral polyps

Tiny builders

Reefs are made by groups of tiny coral animals that live together. Each tiny coral animal is called a polyp. A polyp has a tubelike body and a ring of tentacles around its mouth. A reef is made up of millions of polyps all living together in one colony and held together by the stony skeleton.

Living in crevices

Many animals, such as the moray eel, hide in the cracks and crevices on the reef. The moray eel darts out and grabs any small fish that swim too close.

Feather star

Feather stars are related to starfish and live on the coral reef. They have a cup-shaped body and many feathery arms. The arms are covered in a sticky substance that traps small animals as they float by.

Feather star

Hunting fish

Reef sharks are clever hunters. They have found a way of herding shoals of fish against the faces of reefs. The fish cannot swim away, so are more easy to catch and eat.

apper fish live on the reef.
g reef sharks eat fish like this.

Vase sponges

onges

ponges are animals,
t they do not
ove around. Some
onges grow to
out 6.5 feet tall.
thers form a flat,
ustlike growth over
e surface of the reef.
here are more than
000 different types of
onge. Some of the
rgest may be many
ndreds of years old.

REEF SHARKS

Sharks are among the most feared animals on the reef.
Large reef sharks cruise along the reef edge looking for fish,
while smaller sharks hunt shrimps and crabs among the corals.

Blacktip reef shark

Blacktip reef sharks are not hunted by
any other animals. This shark hunts in
shallow water and lagoons. It catches
sea snakes as well as fish and octopuses.

Whitetip reef shark

The whitetip reef shark is browny gray
in color, but has white tips on its fins.
It rests during the day and hunts for food
at night in the crevices of the coral reef.

Zebra sharks

Zebra sharks live on the reef. Adults have
spots, but when they are young they have
stripes, just like a zebra. Their downward-
pointing mouth is designed to pick up
clams from the seabed. They also hunt
crabs and small fish.

A whitetip reef shark
rests under a
coral ledge.

DISCOVERY FACT™

Blacktip reef sharks sometimes bite off the legs of people who are wading through shallow water. Some experts think it is safer to swim through the shallows, rather than wading.

Blacktip reef sharks have distinctive black markings on the ends of their fins.

Gray reef shark

Gray reef sharks are very aggressive fish. If a diver gets too close, the shark will perform a threat display, warning that it is about to attack. It hunches its back and makes a side-to-side movement in the water.

Caribbean reef shark
This torpedo-shaped shark has become a major tourist attraction in the clear waters of the Caribbean Sea. Some experienced scuba divers go there especially to photograph them.

TYPES OF REEF

There are three types of reef: a fringing reef, formed by corals that follow a coastline; a barrier reef, which grows farther away from the land; and a circular reef, called an atoll. Reef sharks live in all three types of reef.

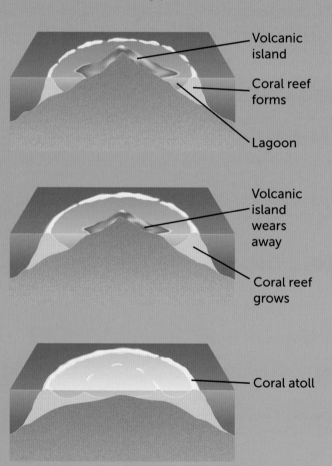

Volcanic island

Coral reef forms

Lagoon

Volcanic island wears away

Coral reef grows

Coral atoll

Coral atoll

Lagoo

How an atoll forms
Atolls take millions of years to form. Volcanoes create islands in the oceans. Then coral animals build reefs around the islands. Over a long time, the volcanic islands wear away, but the reefs keep growing—leaving behind the atoll rings.

Coral atolls
A coral atoll is a ring of coral reef surrounding an area of shallow water, called a lagoon. The coral reef protects the lagoon from the ocean waves. Most of the world's atolls are found in the Indian and Pacific Oceans.

Whitetip and gray reef
sharks prefer clear water.
Whitetip reef sharks like
the water in lagoons, while
gray reef sharks prefer the
deeper waters off
the reef edge.

New coral

Coral polyps like to grow on
something hard. They will even
make their home on the remains
of a sunken ship. Eventually,
the wreck becomes a new
habitat for sharks, smaller fish,
and other marine animals.

oral sand

aves batter against the coral reef,
d the reef gradually wears away.
e tiny particles of coral are washed
 on the shore as sand, eventually
eating beautiful tropical beaches.

A beach with
fine coral sand.

BLACKTIP REEF SHARK

Fast-swimming and active, the blacktip reef shark is one of the three most common sharks inhabiting coral reefs in the tropical waters of the Indian Ocean and the western and central Pacific Ocean. It is mostly found in shallow inshore waters.

These streamlined sharks are brownish-gray on their upper surfaces and white underneath.

They are fast and active hunters, pursuing small fish and invertebrates back and forth around the reef. The patch of water in which they hunt is fairly small in size, and they do not stray far from these home waters, often staying in the same area for years at a time. Most blacktip reef sharks are found near rocky ledges and sandy flats, though they have also been known to swim into brackish (partly salty) water and even into freshwater near the sea.

This shark is fairly timid and does not pose a serious threat to humans. However, it has been known to bite people that come close when swimming, and particularly when wading, in shallow water.

Head
The snout is short and blunt, the eyes are oval, and the mouth is filled with narrow, saw-edged teeth.

Fins
All the fins have black or dark brown tips. This is highlighted on the dorsal fin, which has a light band beneath it.

Profile

Length:	5.2–5.9 ft (males and females)
Weight:	Up to 31 lb maximum (males and females)
Order:	Ground sharks
Family:	Requiem sharks
Diet:	Small fish, squid, shrimps, octopuses (right)

Tail
A sickle-shaped tail fin, built for speed, propels the blacktip reef shark through the water.

Location

Blacktip reef sharks are found in the shallow tropical (more than 64 °F) waters of the Indian and Pacific Oceans and the eastern Mediterranean Sea. They swim from the shallows to about 230 feet deep.

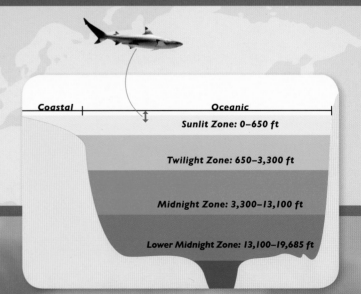

Coastal | Oceanic

Sunlit Zone: 0–650 ft

Twilight Zone: 650–3,300 ft

Midnight Zone: 3,300–13,100 ft

Lower Midnight Zone: 13,100–19,685 ft

HARD CORALS

Hard corals are those with limestone skeletons. There are many different species of hard coral, each forming an interesting shape on the reef.

Table coral
Table coral is a fast-growing, spreading coral that forms a flat, table-like shape. It grows to several feet across and is made up of lots of short branches.

Mushroom coral
The mushroom coral is round or oval in shape. It can be flat or domed and is usually about 18 inches across. Most corals are made up of many polyps, but this type has just one large one.

Table coral

Black coral

rain coral is shaped like a ball
th furrows on its surface.

rain coral

rain coral gets its name
om the way it looks like
e folded surface of a real
ain. These corals grow
o to 5.9 feet tall and are
rong enough to survive
rough seas.

lack coral

ack corals are found
deeper water, where
ere is less light. They are
ranching corals, which look
little like bushes with small
ranches. The skeleton is
ack, but the polyps are
hite, yellow, or orange.

DISCOVERY FACT™

Black coral is in danger
of dying out because too
much has been collected. It
is made into jewelry. Some
divers risk diving very deep
to gather black coral that
they can sell.

CARIBBEAN REEF SHARK

The Caribbean reef shark is one of the most common sharks in the Caribbean. It is most active at night when it hunts for fish and invertebrates to eat.

A Caribbean reef shark has the muscular, streamlined shape that is typical of requiem sharks. It has a dark gray to gray-brown back, and white to light yellow stomach.

Caribbean reef sharks live near coral reefs and ocean bottoms near the continental and island shelves. They prefer shallow waters with a maximum depth of 100 feet. They are often found on the outer edges of coral reefs and sometimes even lying motionless on the ocean floor.

They feed mainly on small fish, which they grasp in the corner of the mouth. They use a sudden sideways snap of the jaws.

Some people stage shark feeds for tourists. Critics claim that this changes the natural balance of the food chain—the sharks may start to see humans as reliable sources of food, increasing the chances of a shark attack on humans.

Fins
The tips of the lower fins are dark, as are the rear edges of the large tail fin.

Profile

Length:	5–5.5 ft (males) and up to 10 ft (females)
Weight:	Up to 154 lb maximum (males and females)
Order:	Ground sharks
Family:	Requiem sharks
Diet:	Fish including rays, invertebrates such as octopuses and squid

Eyes
Large and circular eyes, with protective third eyelids that can be drawn across the eyes as protection.

Location
Caribbean reef sharks are found in the shallow tropical (more than 64 °F) waters of the western Atlantic Ocean, as far south as northern Brazil. These streamlined sharks swim from the shallows to about 100 feet deep.

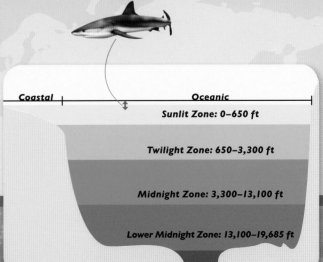

Coastal | Oceanic

Sunlit Zone: 0–650 ft

Twilight Zone: 650–3,300 ft

Midnight Zone: 3,300–13,100 ft

Lower Midnight Zone: 13,100–19,685 ft

SOFT CORALS

Soft corals come in a wide range of colors, such as red, yellow, orange, and purple. Soft corals are those that do not have a hard skeleton.

DISCOVERY FACT™

Soft coral is known as a flower animal because it can take on many different shapes and colors. The bright colors act as warning signs to fish that the coral is poisonous.

Underwater fans

Fan corals form beautiful fan shapes, up to 10 feet across, which move gently in the currents. Each fan has a flexible stem fixing it firmly to the rocks.

Fan corals are also called sea fans.

Feeding corals

Coral polyps feed by extending their tentacles into the water to catch small animals. The tentacles are covered in stinging cells, which they use to kill their prey and to defend themselves.

Whip coral

Whip corals look a little bit like long straws. They bend in the ocean currents catching plankton to eat, b do not get damaged.

Yellow finger gorgonian coral.

Whip coral has long, whiplike branches covered in tiny polyps.

Fire coral

Fire corals have a powerful sting. This protects the polyps from coral-eating fish. Fire corals are often found on the edge of the reef because they can survive in rough water.

LIVING TOGETHER

Animals live closely together on the reef. Some depend on others for a home, to stay clean, or for protection from predators.

Keeping a balance

Healthy coral reefs need sharks. Without sharks, large reef fish seriously reduce the numbers of algae-eating fish. The coral then suffers because too much algae on a reef kills it.

Cleaning station

Fish have difficulty removing the tiny parasites that live on their body, so they visit "cleaning stations" on the reef. Here, small fish and cleaner shrimps remove and eat the parasites for them.

Caribbean reef shark

Clown fish

Decorator crabs attach sponges and seaweeds to their shell. These living decorations help to disguise the crab from predators.

Living with stings

Anemones are covered in sting cells. Most animals stay away, but not the clown fish. It is able to live safely among the tentacles, as it is covered with a slimy mucus that protects it.

A coral grouper fish is cleaned by cleaner shrimps.

Cleanup

The coral grouper fish opens its mouth so that a cleaner shrimp can remove parasites from every nook and cranny. The shrimp gets a meal, and the fish gets rid of parasites.

Living camouflage

The hermit crab protects its soft body by living inside an empty shell. Anemones have attached themselves to this hermit crab's shell. The anemones provide the crab with camouflage and protection, and in return, the crab helps the anemones to find food.

EATING CORAL

Coral is an important source of food for many reef animals, including turtles, starfish, snails, and lots of fish. These eat the coral polyps themselves and also tiny organisms that live within the reef.

Parrot fish
The parrot fish uses its large, beak-like teeth to bite off lumps of coral covered in algae, crunching them into small pieces. Much of the coral passes through its gut and ends up as sand on a beach!

The parrot fish gets its name from its teeth, which look like a parrot's beak.

DISCOVERY FACT™

Overfishing of sharks is causing "desertification" of coral reefs. This is when the coral dies and turns white. Without sharks, the balance of the reef is changed. Huge algae blooms can grow, which stifle the coral.

Hawksbill sea turtle
This sea turtle has a pointe beak like that of a bird. It is perfect for reaching into crevices on the reef to grasp sponges, which are its favorite food.

Butterfly fish

Butterfly fish have a flat body and a long, thin snout. They are the perfect shape to pick up small animals from inside coral crevices. Butterfly fish have colorful patterns—just like butterflies!

Hawksbill sea turtle

Reef devourer

The large crown-of-thorns starfish has a huge appetite for coral. It has up to 18 arms and is covered with poisonous spines. At night, it crawls onto coral and empties its stomach contents. The digestive juices turn the coral into a liquid, which the starfish then sucks up.

One crown-of-thorns starfish can eat up to 140 square feet of coral in a year.

Grey reef shark
The gray reef shark is often found in fairly shallow water around reefs in the tropical waters of the Indian and western and central Pacific Oceans. They grow to around 6.5 feet long and feed mainly on fish and mollusks, such as squid and octopuses.

HUNTERS ON THE REEF

Sharks are not the only predators on the reef. Barracuda, octopuses, and lion fish are also attracted to the thousands of fish and small animals living on the reef.

Reef sharks are apex predators—they are not preyed upon by other predators.

Barracuda

The barracuda has powerful jaws, knife-like teeth, and a long body. It hangs in the water without moving, then darts forward to grab prey with a burst of speed.

Lion fish

This is a dangerous fish—its spines are tipped with poison. Lion fish trap prey using their large, spiny fins—and then swallow it whole.

Lion fish

Reef octopus

The reef octopus hides in holes with just its legs sticking out. It grabs its prey of fish or clams with its suckers and pulls it toward its mouth. The octopus then uses its powerful beak to crush its meal.

WHITETIP REEF SHARK

One of the most common sharks found around coral reefs in the Indian and Pacific Oceans, the whitetip reef shark is typically found on or near the bottom in clear water.

During the day, whitetip reef sharks spend much of their time resting inside caves or even out in the open, lying on the seabed. Unlike other requiem sharks, which must constantly swim to breathe, the whitetip can lie still on the bottom without fear of drowning, as it can pump water over its gills.

At night, whitetips start to hunt. Their bodies are ideal for wriggling their way into gaps in the reef in pursuit of fish. They sometimes break off pieces of the coral in their eagerness to snatch the prey. Their target fish are beyond the reach of other species of shark that feed in open water. For this reason, whitetips are able to live alongside other species of reef shark without competing for the same sources of food.

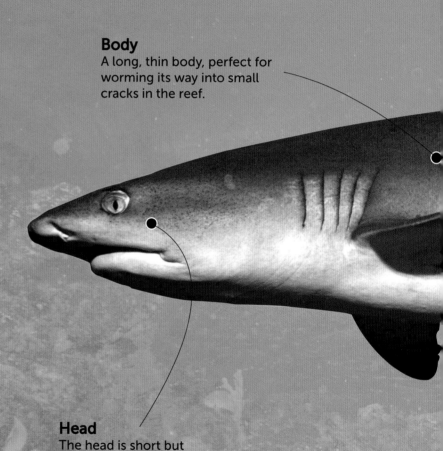

Body
A long, thin body, perfect for worming its way into small cracks in the reef.

Head
The head is short but broad, with whisker-like skin flaps beside the nostrils, called barbels.

Profile

Length:	3.6–5.2 ft (males and females)
Weight:	Up to 40 lb maximum (males and females)
Order:	Ground sharks
Family:	Requiem sharks
Diet:	Fish, octopuses, crabs, spiny lobsters (right)

Fins
Prominent white tips on the first dorsal fin and the tail fin give the whitetip reef shark its name.

Location
Whitetip reef sharks are found in the shallow tropical and subtropical (more than 64 °F) waters of the Indian and Pacific Oceans and along the western coast of Central America. They swim from the shallows to about 130 feet deep.

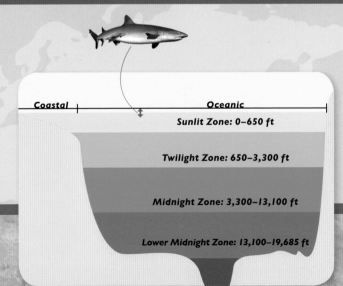

Coastal | Oceanic

Sunlit Zone: 0–650 ft

Twilight Zone: 650–3,300 ft

Midnight Zone: 3,300–13,100 ft

Lower Midnight Zone: 13,100–19,685 ft

REEF DEFENSE

Reef animals protect themselves from predators, such as sharks, in different ways. Some use body armor or poisons to defend themselves. Others rely on camouflage to keep them hidden on the reef.

Hiding in coral

Corals make great hiding places for the creatures that live on them. To escape from the many kinds of predator that are trying to eat them, they can hide in the thousands of cracks and crevices that are part of the reef structure.

Body armor

Seahorses use body armor to defend themselves. The tough armor gives them good protection, but makes swimming more difficult. They stay still much of the time, relying on their camouflage to hide them from hungry hunters.

Frog camouflage

Frog fish look more like a piece of coral or sponge than a fish. By keeping perfectly still, they blend in with the reef and are difficult for predators to spot.

Hide and seek

Tiny animals, such as this small goby, hide from their predators on and among the coral branches. The smallest gobies are less than half an inch long.

The reef stonefish is one of the most poisonous fish in the world. It has 13 spines, which inject poison into anything that touches them.

Spiny defense

The cowfish's spiky body armor, with long spines over each eye, gives it an unusual appearance. If the cowfish is attacked, it can also release a poison into the water from its skin.

Reef stonefish look like a lump of rock or coral. This is wonderful camouflage.

Blacktip reef shark
Blacktips like to stay in a fairly small area of water. They spend most of the time swimming back and forth along the edges of a reef, looking for their prey—mainly small fish.

OUT AT NIGHT

The reef is active at night because many of the animals are nocturnal. They hide during the day in caves and crevices, then come out to feed in the safety of the dark.

Cardinal fish

Whitetip reef shark

This shark mostly rests during the day, often lying with other whitetips. It becomes active at night when it hunts for food. It likes prey that live on the seabed in caves and crevices in the reef, especially octopuses, crabs, lobsters, fish, and eels.

Cardinal fish

The female cardinal fish lays her eggs in the water, where they are fertilized by the male. The male then collects them in his mouth and cares for them until they hatch. He releases the young fish in the safety of darkness.

Safety in numbers

Snappers are seen at night swimming around in small groups. They hunt crabs, shrimps, worms, and fish that live on sandy seabeds near reefs.

DISCOVERY FACT™

The whitetip reef shark's thick skin protects it from getting cuts and grazes when bumping into the sharp coral.

Whitetip reef shark

Squirrel fish

Squirrel fish have extra-large eyes to help them see in low light conditions. The fish hide in caves and wrecked ships by day, then they come out at night to feed on plankton.

REEF MOLLUSKS

Mollusks are a group of animals that include snails, clams, and squid. Most mollusks have a muscular "foot," which they use to move around.

Nudibranches live on the seabed.

Giant clam

The giant clam is a bivalve—a snail with two shells that are hinged together. Clams stay in one place on the reef, sucking water into their body and filtering out plankton. Their color comes from algae, which live in their cells and provide the clams with food.

Nudibranch

Nudibranches are soft-bodied sea slugs that have no shell. Without a shell for protection, they use poison to defend themselves against predators. They are brightly colored to warn other animals that they are poisonous.

The giant clam can open and close the two halves of its shell.

DISCOVERY FACT™

The largest giant clams grow to more than 3 feet across, weigh more than 440 pounds, and can live for up to 100 years.

Mollusk hunter

The zebra shark hunts mainly at night. It feeds on mollusks that live on the seabed. It will also eat crustaceans, small fish, and even sea snakes. These sharks swim like eels do, waving their body and tail from side to side to move through the water. Adults can grow to around 8.2 feet long.

Coral eaters

These flamingo tongue snails are coral eaters. As they crawl over the coral, their feet release digestive juices. The juices dissolve the polyps, and the snails absorb the nutrients through their foot.

ell protection

heavy shell, such as this
lmet shell, protects the
ft body of a snail. When
reatened, the snail retreats
o its shell.

The shell of a tongue snail is white. The spots are on a thin soft layer that covers the shell.

OCEAN SHARKS

Stretching beyond the coastal waters is the vast open ocean. It covers thousands of square miles of the Earth's surface and extends down for thousands of feet. Many different marine animals live in these huge stretches of water, including some of the strangest-looking, fiercest, and most amazing sharks of all.

SURFACE WATERS

The open oceans are home to fewer animals than coral reefs and coastal waters. Most animals that do live here are found in the surface layer, which is the top 650 feet.

During storms at sea, it is not unusual for waves to reach more than 100 feet in height. That is as tall as a 10-story building!

Light in the water

The ocean's surface is lit by sunlight. The top 100 feet is brightly lit, but it gets darker as you go deeper. By 650 feet, all sunlight has gone, and the water looks blue-black.

Surface waves

When the wind blows over the surface of the ocean, it creates waves. As the waves grow larger, they are moved along by the wind, and this helps to mix up the water.

Countershading

Many sharks have dark backs and white stomachs. This is called countershading. From above, their dark backs blend with the depths of the water below. From below, their light stomachs blend with the sunlight coming from above.

e wind blowing over the
rface of the sea pushes
ng wind-powered
ats, such as this yacht.

Flying fish

The flying fish has an unusual way of escaping
predators. When threatened, it swims straight
at the surface of the water and flies into the air,
using its fins like wings. It can glide above the
surface for up to 330 feet.

FLOATING LIFE

The surface layer is home to many floating animals, both large and small. These are carried across the ocean by the currents and waves.

Food source

The tiny plants and animals that float near the surface attract whales and sharks that eat them. The whales and sharks migrate long distances to follow this source of food.

Tiny hunters

The larvae of squid and fish are found in the surface layer, where they drift in the currents. These tiny larvae hunt even smaller animals, such as copepods and amphipods.

DISCOVERY FACT™

To breathe, most oceanic sharks must keep swimming forward in order to force seawater through their open mouths and over their gills—otherwise they would suffocate.

Siphonophores

Siphonophores are formed from a colony of individual polyps—each with a different job to do. Their long, stinging tentacles dangle in the water to catch fish and shrimps.

After making deep dives, whale sharks usually return to the surface to warm up.

Floating stings

The Portuguese man-of-war looks like a jellyfish, but it is a siphonophore. One polyp floats above the surface to catch the wind. Others form hanging tentacles to trap food.

WHALE SHARK

This is a true giant—the largest fish in the ocean. Despite its name, it is not a whale, but a gigantic shark that cruises slowly through the sea sucking in vast amounts of water as it filter-feeds.

The whale shark has distinctive light-yellow markings (random stripes and spots) dotted across its skin. Its skin can be up to 4 inches thick. The underlying color is usually dark gray, blue, or brown. Three large ridges run down each side of its body.

These sharks live in warm water, normally out in the open sea, although they do also come fairly close to shore. They are usually solitary feeders, swimming near the surface, where they scoop up vast amounts of plankton and small fish in their huge mouths. These are sieved out from the water using a technique called filter-feeding.

Whale sharks are quite harmless to humans. They are not worried by scuba divers coming close to them in the water.

Mouth
A huge gaping mouth vacuums up plankton and small fish.

Profile

Length:	20–40 ft (males and females)
Weight:	Typically around 16.5 tons (males and females), 22.5 tons maximum
Order:	Carpet sharks
Family:	Whale sharks
Diet:	Plankton (right), small fish, crustaceans

Gill slits
Large bristly gill rakers, behind each gill slit, filter particles of food from the water.

Location

Whale sharks are found worldwide in tropical (more than 64 °F) and warm temperate (50–64 °F) waters. They swim from the surface to 2,300 feet deep.

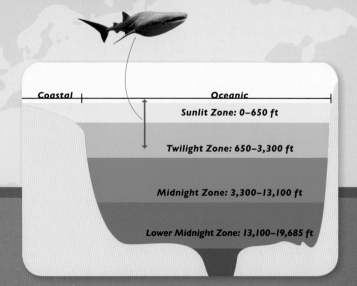

Coastal | Oceanic

Sunlit Zone: 0–650 ft

Twilight Zone: 650–3,300 ft

Midnight Zone: 3,300–13,100 ft

Lower Midnight Zone: 13,100–19,685 ft

JELLYFISH

Few marine animals will try to eat jellyfish because their sting is so painful. But some big fish, including tiger sharks, do eat them. They can swallow them without being hurt by the stings.

Jellyfish are not actually fish—they are related to corals and sea anemones. They are invertebrates with a soft, bell-shaped body with tentacles hanging beneath the bell. Each tentacle is covered in cells that can sting or kill other creatures.

Some jellyfish are so poisonous that they are a danger to humans. Each year, more people are killed by jellyfish than by great white sharks.

Most jellyfish float in the water and are carried around by currents. Some can swim very slowly by squeezing water in and out of their bell—which looks like an umbrella opening and closing. This movement sends pulses of water out of the back of the jellyfish, causing it to move forward.

Mauve stinger jellyfish are found mainly in warm waters in the open ocean.

Lion's mane

The largest jellyfish is the lion's mane. Its bell is more than 3 feet across, and the tentacles are many yards long. They eat almost anything that bumps into their tentacles.

Sea nettles

Sea nettles are a small type of jellyfish. Each year, in some parts of the world, swarms of sea nettles gather together to lay eggs. Sea nettles can sting, so people and marine animals stay away from these areas.

DISCOVERY FACT™

Jellyfish have been around for more than 650 million years, which means that they are older than both dinosaurs and sharks.

SHOALS OF FISH

Many fish live together in groups called shoals. Some shoals contain just a few fish, but when shoals join togethe a huge shoal of hundreds of thousands of fish may form.

Living in groups

Fish are safer in large groups. A shoal of fish confuses hunters by darting around in different directions. The fish use their senses to make sure that they do not bump into each other.

Sardines form huge shoals that attract hunters such as sharks, dolphins, and swordfish.

Working as a team

Sharks sometimes work together to hunt shoals of fish. They scare the fish into a tight ball and then attack the trapped prey.

Bigeye jacks

These fish are powerful hunters with large eyes and a forked tail. They patrol the oceans in large shoals seeking out smaller fish, which they catch in their large jaws. These fish can grow up to 3.3 feet long.

A shoal of fish moves away from an approaching diver.

DISCOVERY FACT™

During the 1970s, enormous herring shoals of more than three billion fish were thought to exist in the North Atlantic Ocean.

BLUE SHARK

The blue shark is a long-distance traveler. It swims hundreds of miles every year, searching for food or to mate.

The blue shark has a bright blue back and a white stomach—these colors help to hide it in the ocean. Viewed from above, the deep blue blends with the murky waters; viewed from below, the white helps the shark to blend in with the light coming from above.

These large sharks hunt with their mouths wide open, trapping small fish, such as sardines, in their jaws. They also feed on squid and other invertebrates, such as octopuses and cuttlefish.

Blue sharks are slow swimmers but can move very quickly when attacking their prey. They travel long distances in their widespread habitat. One blue shark made a trip of over 4,000 miles from New York to Brazil!

Eyes
Large eyes are protected by a transparent third eyelid, which the shark can flick over the eyeball when it is hunting.

Tail
A long tail provides swimming power as the tail moves side-to-side.

Pectoral fins
Long pectoral fins— the same length as the distance between the tip of the snout and the last gill slit.

Profile

Length:	5.9–9.1 ft long (males), 7.2–10.8 ft long (females)
Weight:	60–121 lb (males), 205–401 lb (females)
Order:	Ground sharks
Family:	Requiem sharks
Diet:	Bony fish, squid, and other invertebrates

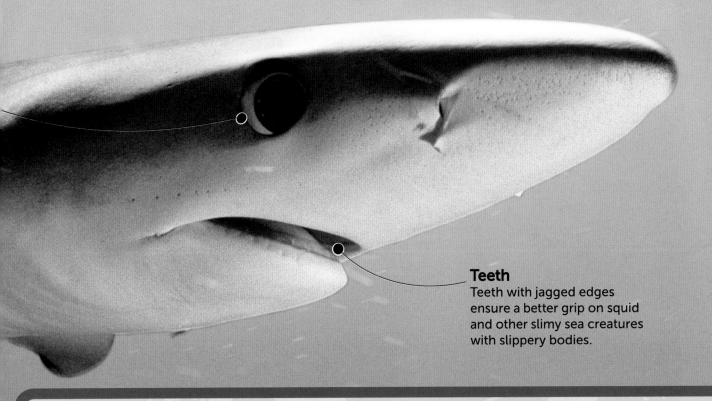

Teeth

Teeth with jagged edges ensure a better grip on squid and other slimy sea creatures with slippery bodies.

Location

Blue sharks are found worldwide in temperate (50–64 °F) waters and at lower depths in tropical (more than 64 °F) waters. They swim from the surface to about 1,150 feet deep.

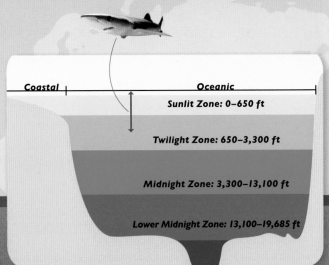

Coastal | Oceanic

Sunlit Zone: 0–650 ft

Twilight Zone: 650–3,300 ft

Midnight Zone: 3,300–13,100 ft

Lower Midnight Zone: 13,100–19,685 ft

SQUID

Squid are an important link in the ocean food chain. It is a hunter of smaller animals, such as krill and fish, and is itself the prey of hunters such as sharks, swordfish, and dolphins.

A squid has eight arms and two longer tentacles. When it gets close to its prey, it shoots out its long tentacles to grab the animal and pull it into its mouth.

To move along, a squid draws water into its body and then forces it out through a funnel on its belly. This creates a powerful jet of water that pushes the squid backward through the water. It can also move its fins to help it swim along.

DISCOVERY FACT™

Large squid can move at 18 miles per hour, faster than many ships can travel. But they can only go this fast in short bursts, when chasing food or escaping from a predator.

This squid has caug[ht] a fish in its tentacle[s]

Squid have small suckers that cover the underside of the arms.

rge eye

uid have large eyes that are very
ilar to human eyes, with a pupil
d a lens. They rely on their sight
ind prey.

Colorful messages

Squid can change the color of their skin. They
can blend into the background or change color
to confuse a predator. Their color reflects their
mood, too. Angry squid are often red. This squid
is bioluminescent—it gives off an eerie glow in
the dark.

GREAT HAMMERHEAD SHARK

There are nine species of hammerhead sharks, and the great hammerhead is the biggest of them. The shape of their head is unique.

Great hammerhead sharks are gray-brown to olive green on top with an off-white underside.

No one knows for sure why their head has such a strange shape. Scientists think that the extra distance between its eyes gives the shark a huge field of vision both above and below. Masses of special sensors on the underside of the "hammer" may allow it to detect the presence of stingrays when they are lying buried in the sand on the sea floor. Some hammerheads have even been seen to pin a stingray to the sea floor with their heads while they take a bite out of its wings to stop it escaping.

Great hammerheads migrate—they head to warmer waters during the winter and then return to their normal feeding grounds in summer.

Dorsal fin
A tall and pointed dorsal fin helps to stabilize the shark when it is turning quickly in the water as it hunts for prey.

Head
The head is shaped like a flattened hammer with the eyes set at the edges.

Tail

A tall tail fin made up of a large upper section, called a lobe, and a smaller lower section, propels the shark through the water.

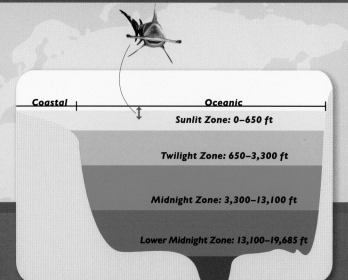

Profile

Length:	13–20 ft (males and females)
Weight:	507–992 lb (males and females)
Order:	Ground sharks
Family:	Hammerhead sharks
Diet:	Fish, including rays (below) and other sharks, squid, octopuses, crustaceans

Location

Great hammerheads are found worldwide in tropical and subtropical (more than 64 °F) waters. They swim from the surface to about 262 feet deep.

Coastal | Oceanic

Sunlit Zone: 0–650 ft

Twilight Zone: 650–3,300 ft

Midnight Zone: 3,300–13,100 ft

Lower Midnight Zone: 13,100–19,685 ft

OCEAN HUNTERS

Large hunting fish, such as sharks, swordfish, sailfish, and marlin, are at the top of the ocean food chain. These fearsome fish are designed for hunting.

Marlin

The marlin is related to the tuna and swordfish. It is a large fish with a spearlike snout. It hunts alone, swimming in the surface waters of the ocean in search of fish and squid.

Sailfish

These fish have a large, sail-like fin along their back. They use it to gather together groups of fish and squid, which they then eat. Sailfish can fold back the fin to create a sleek, streamlined shape for swimming.

DISCOVERY FACT™

Mako sharks are very strong and fierce. Some makos have been known to leap into a fishing boat to try to attack the fisherman.

Mako sharks can leap clear
out of the water when they
are swimming really fast.

Mako shark

The mako is a muscular fish with
a tail fin shaped for speed. It can
swim at up to 31 miles an hour. It
has sharp teeth, which it uses to
grip slippery prey such as tuna
and mackerel.

Swordfish

The swordfish is named for its long, swordlike
snout. It does not spear its prey, but moves its
"sword" from side to side to slice it up. It swims
alone and is often seen leaping out of the water.

Scalloped hammerhead shark
This shark's name comes from the "scallops" along the front edge of its hammer. These are missing on other hammerhead sharks. The eyes and nostrils are at the sides of the hammer.

OCEAN GIANTS

Sharks share the oceans with other giant creatures, such as enormous whales, disk-shaped sunfish, and winged manta rays.

Oceanic whitetip shark

The oceanic whitetip shark grows to about 6.5 feet long. It swims just below the surface, but sometimes sticks its nose out of the water to sniff the air in search of food.

An oceanic whitetip shark with pilot fish swimming alongside it.

Manta ray

A manta ray usually swims slowly through the ocean, but when threatened by predators such as sharks, it leaps out of the water in an attempt to escape.

Humpback whale

The humpback whale can grow up to 52 feet long (the same length as a bus) and weigh approximately 79,400 pounds.

Sunfish

The sunfish has an unusual shape—it is almost circular when seen from the side, with fins sticking out of the top and bottom of its body. Sunfish feed on jellyfish and can weigh more than 4,400 pounds.

SILKY SHARK

This is one of the most common sharks in the open ocean. There are tens of millions of these slim, agile predators living in tropical waters around the world.

The back of the silky shark ranges in color from dark brown to a blue-gray. The underside is generally white, and the lower fins can have dark tips on their underside.

This shark usually hunts on it own and generally attacks fish swimming in open water. It is particularly attracted to tuna and is often seen trailing behind shoals of these fish. Sometimes, when there are lots of fish in the water, silky sharks will hunt together in a pack. They "herd" the shoal toward the surface. Then they slice into the shoal with their mouths open, to trap them in their jaws.

Silky sharks can act aggressively toward humans, but because they are normally found out in the open ocean, they do not often come into contact with divers.

Skin
The skin is smooth to the touch, unlike the skin of other species of sharks, which is rough.

Pectoral fin
Long and curved pectoral fins give the shark lift as it swims through the water.

Dorsal fin
A short, rounded dorsal fin helps the silky shark balance.

Profile

Length:	5.9–6.9 ft (males), 6.9–7.5 ft (females)
Weight:	386–661 lb (males and females), 802 lb maximum
Order:	Ground sharks
Family:	Requiem sharks
Diet:	Fish (right), squid, crustaceans

Location
Silky sharks are found worldwide in tropical and subtropical waters, usually at a temperature of 73 °F or more. They swim from around 59 feet to about 1,640 feet deep.

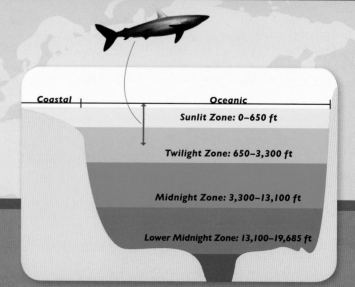

Coastal | Oceanic

Sunlit Zone: 0–650 ft

Twilight Zone: 650–3,300 ft

Midnight Zone: 3,300–13,100 ft

Lower Midnight Zone: 13,100–19,685 ft

OCEAN TURTLES

Many sharks eat turtles, including tiger sharks, great white sharks, short-finned mako sharks, bull sharks, and oceanic whitetip sharks.

Turtles make long journeys across the oceans in search of food. They return to the beach where they were born to lay their eggs. All sea turtles give birth by laying eggs. The female will bury between 50 and 200 eggs (depending on the species) in the sand. After around 60 days, baby turtles hatch out of the eggs. They dig their way out of the sand and instinctively make for the sea.

Turtles spend the first few years of their life in the open ocean. They feed on jellyfish and other animals there before returning to coastal waters to mate.

Green turtle

Green turtles are expert swimmers with a smooth, streamlined shell and flippers. They are the largest hard-shelled turtle in the ocean. They grow to 3 feet across and weigh 440 pounds or more. Baby green turtles are meat-eaters, but adults feed on seagrass.

Turtles have flat flippers to help them swim.

DISCOVERY FACT™

Sharks can get rid of material in their stomachs that they cannot digest, like the turtle's shell, by turning their stomach inside out. The shell is vomited out of the mouth.

All turtles are toothless. Instead of teeth, they use their beak to crush coral and crabs, or graze on seagrass.

Hawksbill turtle

This rare turtle gets its name from the birdlike shape of its head. It spends as long as 20 years at sea before it is ready to breed. Sadly, it is killed for its attractive shell, which is used to make jewelry and ornaments.

OCEANIC WHITETIP SHARK

Oceanic whitetip sharks live in the open ocean. They often follow ships hoping to pick up scraps of food thrown overboard. For this reason, sailors used to call them "sea dogs."

The upper surface of the oceanic whitetip shark's body varies from grayish-bronze to brown in color, depending upon where it is in the world. The underside is whitish, sometimes with a yellow tinge.

The oceanic whitetip usually hunts alone and is quite slow-moving. It tends to cruise in the open ocean near to the surface. It covers vast stretches of empty water scanning for food. However, when it gets near its prey—usually fish or invertebrates—it can put on sudden bursts of speed.

When an oceanic whitetip senses the smell of blood in the water, it may go into a feeding frenzy, swimming around wildly and biting anything that comes near.

Oceanic whitetips are dangerous to humans because of their predatory nature. During World War II, they caused the deaths of many sailors and airmen who found themselves in the water after their ships were sunk or their aircraft were shot down.

Teeth
Sharp triangular upper teeth and smaller pointed lower teeth are ideal for holding and tearing the shark's prey.

orsal fins
is shark has a
, rounded
t fin on
back.

Profile

Length:	5.6–6.2 ft (males), 5.9–6.5 ft (females)
Weight:	77–154 lb (males and females), 368 lb maximum
Order:	Ground sharks
Family:	Requiem sharks
Diet:	Fish, squid and other mollusks, sea turtles, crustaceans

Pectoral fins
Long, paddle-like fins
are set low behind the
gill slits. All the large fins
have white tips.

Location

Oceanic whitetip sharks are found worldwide
in tropical waters, usually at a temperature
between 68 and 82 °F. They swim from the
surface to about 492 feet deep.

Coastal | Oceanic

Sunlit Zone: 0–650 ft

Twilight Zone: 650–3,300 ft

Midnight Zone: 3,300–13,100 ft

Lower Midnight Zone: 13,100–19,685 ft

DOLPHINS

Large species of sharks, such as the great white shark, will eat dolphins, but most sharks do not prey on them. The dolphin is one of the most intelligent animals in the ocean. This playful marine mammal uses sound to find its prey and lives in groups.

Living together

Dolphins live together in groups called pods. A pod usually contains about 10 to 12 dolphins, but superpods of thousands of dolphins are formed when pods join up for a short period. This happens when food is found in great quantities.

Dolphins are athletic swimmers and love to play together.

Hunting with sound

Dolphins use sound to find their prey. This is called echolocation. They make whistling and clicking sounds, which travel through the water. These sound waves bounce off any prey in the water, creating echoes that the dolphins can hear. The echoes tell the dolphin the shape, size, and location of their prey.

DISCOVERY FACT™

In 2004, dolphins saved the lives of four swimmers who were threatened by a great white shark off the coast of New Zealand. The dolphins swam in circles around the people until the shark swam away.

Leaping dolphins

The acrobatic dolphin moves its powerful tail up and down to build up enough speed to jump out of the water. Dolphins often leap into the air while chasing fish to eat. Sometimes they even play chase with other dolphins.

Looking after baby

A female dolphin gives birth to her baby, or calf, underwater. The mother pushes her calf to the surface so it can take its first breath. The calf feeds on its mother's milk for about a year.

Oceanic whitetip shark
The large fins on this ocean shark have made it
a target for fishermen who supply shark fins to the
food industry. These are turned into shark's fin soup.
Unfortunately, this dish is very popular, and whitetip
numbers have fallen dramatically.

SARGASSO SEA

The Sargasso Sea is a huge area of floating seaweed in the Atlantic Ocean. It is home to many animals—some stay all year, but others, like porbeagle sharks, are just visitors.

Sargassum weed

Thick mats of sargassum weed cover much of the Sargasso Sea. This weed is free-floating, not attached to rocks or the seabed. Turtles and fish hide among the mats, while crabs and small shrimps cling to the weed.

Eels

Adult eels swim to the Sargasso Sea to lay their eggs. The young eels hatch and then make their way back to North America and Europe.

Location

The Sargasso Sea covers an area of about 1.15 million square miles. It is an area with slow ocean currents surrounded by fast-moving currents that circulate around the Sargasso Sea in a clockwise direction.

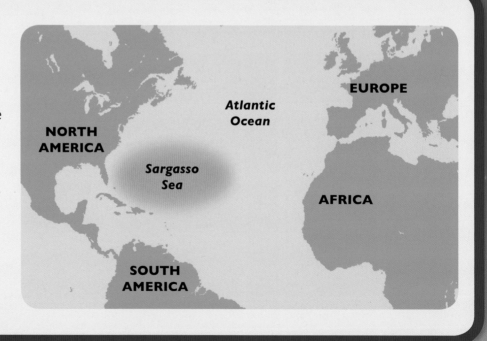

EUROPE

Atlantic Ocean

NORTH AMERICA

Sargasso Sea

AFRICA

SOUTH AMERICA

The vast Sargasso Sea is the only sea in the world that does not have a coastline. Instead, it is bordered by fast-moving water.

...all air sacs
...ep the
...gassum
...ed afloat.

Porbeagle sharks

Female porbeagle sharks migrate south to the Sargasso Sea to give birth to their pups. The young pups and the adult sharks then make their way back to the cooler North Atlantic, where they spend most of the year.

MOVING UP AND DOWN

During the day, the brightly lit surface waters are virtually empty of small animals. Most dive to the safety of the darker water below. They return to feed under the cover of darkness.

Tuna fish prey on smaller fish, which they swallow whole. They follow their prey on its migration to the deeper water.

Nighttime travelers

This daily movement is only a few hundred yards, but for tiny animals, such as shrimps and copepods, it is a long journey. It is the only way to feed in safety.

Shrimp

At sunset, the animals swim up to the surface waters to feed.

At sunrise, the animals swim back down to the dark water.

Mass migration

Most types of plankton and some types of plankton-eating fish migrate up and down, including krill, herring, and mackerel.

At night, the animals feed on plankton.

Lantern fish

Lantern fish travel the greatest distances each day. During the day, they are found more than 5,600 feet down, and at night they rise to within 330 feet of the surface. They get their name from the glowing light organs (called photophores) along their body.

Tiger shark

The tiger shark is one of the largest sharks. It hunts mainly at night when it comes up close to the surface of the water. During the day, it goes deeper down into the ocean, usually to around 1,000 feet.

The tiger shark eats all sorts of marine creatures including dolphins, seals, turtles, fish, and even other sharks.

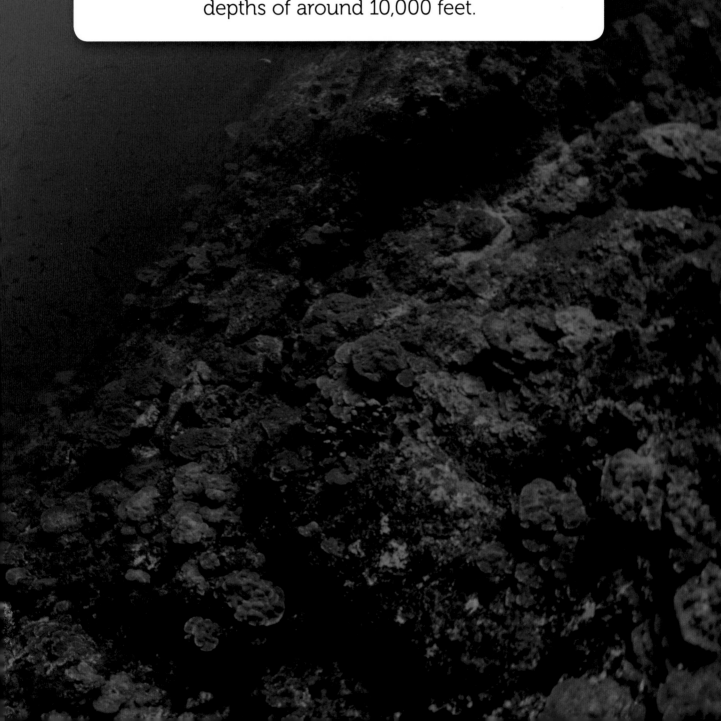

SHARKS IN THE DEEP

Scientists have explored the upper layers of the sea quite thoroughly, but the deep ocean is still a mysterious place. We do not know much about this habitat. Few people have explored it by submarine. However, we do know that sharks live in deep water and can survive down to depths of around 10,000 feet.

GOING DOWN

As you descend from the surface, the sea becomes darker and colder. The pressure increases, too. In very deep water, a diver would be crushed and all the air squeezed from their lungs. Only animals adapted to this environment can survive. The surface layer goes down to about 650 feet. Next comes the twilight zone, from 650 to 3,300 feet. The midnight zone stretches to the seabed.

Sunlit zone

Sunlight passes through the water to depths of about 650 feet. Here in the surface layer, there is enough light for plant plankton and seaweeds to make their food.

Nurse sharks spend most of their time in the sunny surface layer of the sea.

Sixgill sharks are found down near the deep seabed.

Twilight zone

Beneath the surface layer, there is a glimmer of light—just enough for some animals to see. Animals dive down from the surface into this layer for safety.

Midnight zone

The midnight zone is pitch black and cold, and the water is still. Fish and other sea creatures living below 1,640 feet are designed to withstand the great pressure of the surrounding water.

erm whales can stay
derwater for well
r an hour without
ing a breath.

Sperm whales
can dive to incredible
depths. One sperm
whale caught by a
whaling ship in water
10,000 feet deep had a
shark in its stomach.

Coastal	Oceanic	
	Sunlit Zone: 0–650 ft	
	Twilight Zone: 650–3,300 ft	
	Midnight Zone: 3,300–13,100 ft	
	Lower Midnight Zone: 13,100–19,685 ft	

TWILIGHT ZONE

A variety of animals, from tiny plankton to huge whales, live permanently in the twilight zone. Their bodies are specially adapted for life in deep, gloomy water.

Frilled sharks live in deep waters in the twilight zone. They are shaped like a snake, with a huge mouth containing around 300 needle-like teeth.

Cat sharks

Cat sharks are a family of around 150 species. These sharks live in habitats ranging from shallow waters right down to 6,560 feet or more. Some of them hunt in the twilight zone for nautilus, cuttlefish, and squid.

Cat shark

Hatchet fish

A hatchet fish has a flat body. It has light-producing organs on its underside. The lights disguise the fish's shape so that it is not spotted by predators in the water below.

Twilight shrimp

The twilight shrimp has a red shell—a color that is difficult to spot in the gloom. It catches small plankton animals in its claws.

[Na]utilus

[T]he nautilus is a relative of the squid. [It] has a spiral shell for protection. [If] necessary, it can disappear [in]side completely. Its eyes [he]lp it see in [th]e gloom.

The nautilus has many more tentacles than a squid, but no suckers.

Eye

DIVING DEEP

Seals, whales, sharks, and penguins are just some of the animals that dive down into the twilight zone and beyond to find food.

Little is known about the megamouth shark, which was first discovered near Hawaii in 1976. Since then, only about 40 megamouths have been seen.

Megamouth

The odd-looking megamouth shark grows to about 23 feet long. It has a 3-foot-wide mouth. Like many ocean animals, it spends the daylight hours in deep water and swims to the surface to feed at night.

Diving birds

Many seabirds, such as penguins, dive underwater to catch food. The penguin is a flightless bird with flippers rather than wings. It is clumsy on land, but an expert swimmer. The emperor penguin spends up to 15 minutes under the water at a time. It dives to depths of about 1,640 feet.

Weddell seals

The Weddell seal dives at night to find krill, squid, and fish. It can stay under the water for up to an hour, reaching depths of about 2,300 feet before it has to return to the surface to breathe.

Weddell seal

Twilight hunter

The sperm whale dives down to 3,300 feet or more, in search of squid. Scientists believe that the whale produces sound waves to stun its prey.

GOBLIN SHARK

Very little is known about the goblin shark as it lives in the deep ocean. Only about 45 specimens have been studied to date.

Goblin sharks are not often seen because they live in deep water at the bottom of the ocean. They are only seen when they are caught in the fishing nets of deep-sea trawlers. The goblin shark is pink-gray in color because its blood vessels lie close to the surface of the skin and can be seen through it.

It is very dark in the deep ocean, so the goblin shark does not rely on its eyesight to detect prey. Scientists think that special organs on its long snout can detect the faint electrical fields created by other fish and invertebrates when they move. It may also use the snout to dig up fish and crustaceans that are hiding in the sand and silt on the seafloor.

A goblin shark's jaws act like a spring-loaded trap. The teeth and jaws can be catapulted forward, a little like opening a telescope, to snatch a fish from the water. Then they spring back to their normal position.

Body
The body is soft and quite rubbery. The caudal fin is very long compared to the two dorsal fins.

Profile

Length:	7.9–10.5 ft (males), 10–11.5 ft (females)
Weight:	Around 400 lb (males and females), 463 lb maximum
Order:	Mackerel sharks
Family:	Goblin sharks
Diet:	Fish, squid (right) and other mollusks, crustaceans

Snout
The large flattened snout protrudes from the top of its head. Beneath this are the jaws with slender, fanglike teeth.

Location

Goblin sharks have been found off the coast of Japan, Australia, New Zealand, and southern Africa, and in the eastern Atlantic and Indian Oceans. They swim near the sea bottom at about 820 feet deep, but they can go down to 1,650 feet or more.

Coastal | Oceanic

Sunlit Zone: 0–650 ft

Twilight Zone: 650–3,300 ft

Midnight Zone: 3,300–13,100 ft

Lower Midnight Zone: 13,100–19,685 ft

THE DEEP

The deep is a cold, eerie place where very little lives. The animals of the deep have all kinds of unusual features that help them get something to eat in this "food desert."

Light in the dark

Sunlight does not penetrate the deep ocean. It is very dark all the time. Many animals in the deep-sea have developed organs that can produce light. This is known as bioluminescence. It is used to lure prey, to distract predators, and to attract mates.

The firefly squid has tiny organs on its tentacles that emit light. This attracts small fish, which the squid eats.

Deep-sea medusa

The deep-sea medusa is a relative of the jellyfish. It traps prey, such as small shrimps and baby fish, in its long tentacles. It has 22 of them around its body.

Snipe eel

The snipe eel has jaws that do not close. It swims with its mouth open. Small animals, such as amphipods (shrimplike creatures), are trapped on the teeth and swallowed. The snipe eel grows to over 3 feet long.

Scuba divers do not normally go deeper than around 131 feet. To explore the deep ocean, scientists use manned submersibles or robot vehicles.

DISCOVERY FAC

The velvet bel
shark can g
light. Its phot
(light-producir
are arranged ir
pattern. This h
bellies recog
another in th

Fishing the deep

The anglerfish lures its prey with a light that dangles from the end of a spine in front of its large mouth. The light is produced by tiny bacteria.

DEEP-SEA SQUID

Many stories have been written about monsters of the deep. In these tales, it is said that they have risen from the deep and wrapped their tentacles around boats to pull them down under the water.

One of the most mysterious of the deep-sea squids is the giant squid. These animals are rare, and few have been seen alive.

Sometimes, the bodies of giant squid are washed up on beaches. This gives scientists the chance to study them. Their remains have also been found in the stomachs of sperm whales.

Many giant squid can produce their own light. They switch this light on and off to attract fish. When the fish are close enough, the squid grab them.

The body of a giant squid washed up on a beach.

Colossal squid

The colossal squid is even larger than the giant squid. It is the world's largest invertebrate animal, reaching a massive 46 feet in length. Its tentacles have razor-like hooks, which can cause injuries to other animals.

This deep-sea squid, called *Teuthowenia*, produces its own light to attract prey.

Sleeper sharks

Sleeper sharks live in the cold waters near the North and South Poles. Some of the larger species eat giant squid and colossal squid. The sperm whale is the only other animal known to eat these huge squid.

LIFE ON THE SEABED

Some of the deep seabed is rocky, but it is mostly covered by a thick layer of mud. This mud contains the remains of dead animals that have dropped from the water above.

Pacific sleeper shark

The Pacific sleeper shark feeds on bottom-dwelling fish, shrimps, crabs, and marine snails. Larger sharks can even catch fast-swimming squid, octopuses, salmon, and porpoises.

Deep-sea spines

The round sea urchin is covered in long spines. Its mouth is on the underside, surrounded by five teethlike plates. It uses these plates to feed on dead matter and animals such as mussels and sponges.

ea slug

ea slugs are
nollusks with
 tube-shaped body,
eathery skin, and a ring
f sticky tentacles around its mouth.
 uses its tentacles to find food in the mud.

Sea pens are
related to corals.

Long-legged crabs

Spider crabs scuttle across the deep seabed in search
of food. They have a small body and 10 very long
legs. They cannot see anything in the dark, so they
use their sense of touch to catch prey.

DISCOVERY FACT™

The sea pen attaches to
the deep seabed, where it
catches small animals with
its stinging tentacles. Each
sea pen is actually a colony
of individual polyps that
live together.

SIXGILL SH...

This big shark normally lives in the deep oceans at depths down to...

The sixgill shark ranges in color from gray and olive green to brown on the upper side, fading to a paler underside. There is a light-colored stripe along each flank. It has small, teardrop-shaped, green eyes with black pupils.

It normally hunts on its own, swimming slowly and steadily through the water searching for food. When it spots something to eat, it accelerates rapidly to catch its prey. The teeth in its lower jaw are shaped like the blade of a saw. The shark uses them to rip the flesh off the body of large fish that it cannot swallow whole.

Sixgill sharks are not considered dangerous to humans because they are quite shy and not aggressive unless provoked. Also, they generally keep to deep waters where divers cannot follow them.

Gills
Most sharks have five gill slits on each side of their bodies, but the sixgill shark has six long slits.

Length:	10–10.8 ft long (males), 11.5–14 ft long (females)
Weight:	Average 440 lb (males), 880 lb (females), 1,300 lb maximum
Order:	Frilled and cow sharks
Family:	Cow sharks
Diet:	Fish, snails, crabs (right), shrimps, squid, some marine mammals

Dorsal fin
There is only one dorsal fin on this shark's back, set quite a long way back toward the tail.

Location

Sixgill sharks are found worldwide in tropical (over 64 °F) and temperate (50–64 °F) waters. They usually swim from about 295 feet to as deep as 6,560 feet.

Coastal | Oceanic

Sunlit Zone: 0–650 ft

Twilight Zone: 650–3,300 ft

Midnight Zone: 3,300–13,100 ft

Lower Midnight Zone: 13,100–19,685 ft

DEEP-SEA WORMS

Worms are invertebrate animals with a long, soft, boneless body. There are all kinds of marine worms, including tapeworms and fan worms. Sharks and rays that live near the seabed feed on worms.

Undersea parasites

Parasites are animals that live in, and do harm to, other animals. The tapeworm is a common parasite in many deep-sea fish. The tapeworm lives and feeds in the fish's gut. Tapeworms spread when their eggs are eaten by small creatures, such as crustaceans. These are part of the food chain and are eaten in turn by larger fish. Eventually, a shark will eat the fish that contains the tapeworm parasites and become infected itself.

Blue sharks commonly have parasites inside them.

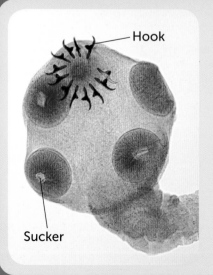

Hook

Sucker

Tapeworms

Tapeworms are parasites that live inside the guts of all types of shark. Tapeworms use their hooks and suckers to grip the inside of the gut, where they absorb food. When the guts of 24 dead blue sharks were cut open, scientists found that each shark contained hundreds of tapeworms inside its guts.

Tube worm

The tentacles of this deep-sea worm look a little bit like spaghetti. The worm extends these sticky tentacles over the seabed to catch any small particles that sink down from above. If danger threatens, the worm pulls the tentacles back into its body.

Catching food

Fan worms are found on the deep seabed. Their soft body is protected by a hard, bony tube. They extend a ring of sticky tentacles from the top of the tube to catch small animals drifting in the water. If disturbed, fan worms can shoot back inside their tubes.

DISCOVERY FACT™

Sometimes, parasites can do good. Worms in the gut of whitecheek sharks absorb high doses of toxic metals such as cadmium and lead. So the worms are filtering out these poisons before they harm the sharks.

FOOD AND SHELTER

When the body of a large animal drops to the seabed, scavengers come from far and wide to feed upon it. Other animals take shelter among objects that find their way to the seabed.

There is a constant supply of "marine snow" from the waters above. This "snow" is the broken-down remains of dead plants and animals—especially plankton. These tiny remains drift slowly to the seabed where they become an important source of food for bottom-dwellers.

Spiny dogfish shark

Finding shelter

Animals on the seabed need shelter from predators. Many hide among bones—or even old cans and objects that have dropped to the seabed. Unfortunately, deep-sea trawling nets can sweep away these tiny shelters.

DISCOVERY FACT™

Sharks usually eat live prey rather than scavenging on the seafloor. But the spiny dogfish shark is a bottom-dwelling scavenger. It has two sharp poisonous spines on its back to keep other predators away.

Hagfish

The hagfish looks something like an eel. It is a scavenger that lives on the ocean floor. The hagfish burrows into the bodies of dead animals and eats them from the inside out. It is an unusual fish because it does not have jaws or teeth. Instead, it has a very rough tongue.

Brittle star

The brittle star has five long arms, which it uses to pull itself across the seabed. It sometimes preys on small shrimps and other animals, but it mostly scavenges on dead matter.

STARFISH

Starfish are spiny-skinned animals that belong to a group of animals called echinoderms. They are related to sea urchins, sea cucumbers, sea stars, and brittle stars.

Most starfish have five or more arms, called rays, joined to a central body. The mouth is on the underside. Starfish eat by pouring the acid from their stomach onto their food. The acid dissolves the food so the starfish can digest it.

To move, a starfish swings each ray forward then pushes down, pulling itself along. There is a tiny sucker at the end of each ray that acts as a grip. The starfish also uses the sucker to force open the shells of mussels and clams.

If a starfish loses one of its rays, it can grow a new one. This process is called regeneration.

Sensing light and dark

Starfish do not have eyes like fish do, but they have eyespots at the end of each ray. These are primitive sensors that can detect light and dark.

Starfish can regrow their rays.

Horn sharks

Bottom-dwelling species such as horn sharks eat starfish. The horn shark uses its front teeth to grab the starfish, then crushes it with its back teeth before swallowing it.

Starfish move slowly, which makes them easy prey for sharks, squid, and octopuses.

Frilled shark

The frilled shark is a strange serpent-like shark that grows to over 3 feet long. It lives in the deep sea, often at depths below 3,300 feet. It has around 300 spearlike teeth that it uses to grasp slippery squid. It gets its name from the frilly edges to its six rows of gills.

SEABED FISH

A surprising number of fish are found on the deep seabed, and more are being discovered all the time. They have been given unusual names such as the rat-tail, cookiecutter shark, and even the blobfish.

The cookiecutter shark has a bioluminescent patch on its belly. Hunting fish think it is harmless since they can only see the small patch in the dark. When they come close, the cookiecutter ambushes them.

Cookiecutter shark

This shark was first discovered off the coast of Brazil in the 1820s. It lives in deep water below 3,300 feet. It gets its name from the round scars that it leaves on its prey. It grips its prey in its mouth and, using its long teeth, pulls out a lump of flesh, leaving behind a nasty hole.

Deep-sea blob

The blobfish was discovered in 2003, on a seabed 1,650 feet deep. Little is known about it, but the shape of its mouth suggests that it eats whatever it can find.

The blobfish lives in deep waters off the coast of Australia.

Sixgill shark

The sixgill shark is found at depths of up to 6,560 feet, where it rests during the day. At night, it swims to the surface to hunt for fish and seals.

Sixgill shark

Deep-sea rat-tail

The rat-tail, or grenadier, is one of the most common deep-sea fish. It has a large head, a slender body and, unusually, no tail fin. These fish live in waters up to 16,400 feet deep, where they hunt animals such as smaller fish and shrimps.

DEEP-OCEAN CLIFFS

There are cliffs, mountains, and trenches in the deep ocean.
These are home to many animals, including corals and sponges.

Deep-sea coral

Not all corals are found in
shallow, warm, tropical seas.
Many corals live in cold,
deep water. Some live as
deep as 3,300 feet. Deep-sea
reefs grow very slowly,
and some are hundreds of
years old.

Deep-sea coral

Deep-sea sponges

Some deep-water
sponges have a skeleton
that is made from glass.
They produce tiny
pieces of glass, which
stick together to form a
beautiful skeleton that
is strong enough to
support their body.

Hiding in cracks

The wolffish, or sea wolf, pushes its body
backward into the cracks of a cliff. It leaves
its head sticking out, watching for prey. It has a
wide mouth with large pointed teeth, which it
uses to feed on clams, mussels, and starfish.

A wolffish hides in a
hole in the rocks.

Cliff hugger

Sea anemones, and other animals that cannot swim, cling tightly to the cliff. If they let go, they could sink into the deep below.

ivers can explore cliffs
at lie close to the surface.
ini-submarines are
eeded for the deep ocean.

DISCOVERY FACT™

The Portuguese shark holds the world record for the deepest-caught shark. Most live at around 3,300 feet, but several have been caught down at around 9,840 feet.

SHARKS AND PEOPLE

Although sharks have been living in the Earth's oceans for more than 400 million years, in recent years their future has become threatened. This is because human beings have started to affect what happens to creatures in the ocean, leading to a serious decline in the number of sharks.

SHARK FISHING

Many sharks are known as apex predators. This means that they kill and eat other animals, but that virtually no predators in the oceans kill them. However, sharks do have one deadly enemy that lives on land—humans.

Commercial fishing

Every year, around 100 million sharks are caught and killed. This is because a lot of people earn their living by catching sharks. Shark products, including meat, the fins, the skin, and the teeth, are sold in huge quantities.

Unwanted victims

Sharks are often caught in trawler nets or on longline hooks that have been set to catch other fish, such as tuna or swordfish. The sharks die, even though the fisherman do not want them. They are known as "by-catch."

Sport fishing

In certain parts of the world, the sport of fishing for big game fish is very popular. Some fishermen release the fish after it has been caught and photographed, but others kill their catch to keep as a trophy.

Sharks are one of the game fish that sport fisherman try to catch using fast boats like this.

Shark's fin soup

A thick soup made from shark fins is very popular in the Far East. It is thought to have medicinal properties. Some fishermen catch sharks, cut off their fins, and then throw the sharks back in the water. Millions die in this way.

GETTING CLOSE TO SHARKS

Many people are curious about sharks—they are big, powerful, and fascinating animals. There are different ways that we can see them up-close.

Diving with sharks

In the clear, warm waters of the tropics, diving with sharks has become a tourist attraction. Some dive companies even organize shark feeds to attract sharks to a particular spot.

In the aquarium

One way that people can get close to sharks is to visit one of the many aquariums that display them to the public. As well as providing a tourist attraction, these sea life centers allow scientists to study shark behavior in order to help protect them.

DISCOVERY FACT™

The Ocean Voyager tank at Georgia Aquarium in Atlanta, Georgia, is the largest aquarium habitat in the world. It contains more than 6 million gallons of salt water—large enough to be a home for whale sharks.

Shark cages

The great white shark is seen as the ultimate man-eater. It is now possible for tourists to watch great whites from inside the safety of a submerged metal cage.

Great white shark

On the screen

Television has had a huge impact on our knowledge of sharks. Nature programs give us an insight into their behavior and habits. Movies such as *Jaws* and *Deep Blue Sea* portray the shark as a deadly monster.

Divers can take photographs of huge sharks while safe inside the cage.

GREAT WHITE SHARK

The huge and aggressive great white is the most dangerous shark in the world. It has attacked more swimmers, surfers, divers, and small boats than any other species of shark.

A great white shark's body is streamlined and shaped like a torpedo. Despite its name, only its belly is actually white; the top is gray or blue-gray. This is useful when hunting its prey because the great white usually strikes from below—to its prey above, its gray color blends in with the dark water.

The shark's target is normally attacked in a surprise rush and bitten once to stun it. Sometimes, the shark will leap out of the water because of the speed and power of its attack. When the victim is stunned and dying, the shark returns to feed.

The great white is the only shark that pokes its head out of the water. It may be to spot prey swimming on the surface, such as seals and sea lions.

Pectoral fins
Large sickle-shaped pectoral fins help the shark to steer through the water.

Profile

Length:	11.5–13 ft (males), 15–16.5 ft (females), 22 ft maximum
Weight:	Average 1,500–4,000 lb (males and females), 7,000 lb maximum
Order:	Mackerel sharks
Family:	Mackerel sharks
Diet:	Fish including other sharks, seals, sea lions, dolphins, small whales, sea turtles

Nostrils
An incredible sense of smell can detect one drop of blood in 26 gallons of water and sense blood up to 3 miles away.

Teeth
Around 300 huge, triangular, jagged teeth—each one as long as a human finger.

Location
Great white sharks are found worldwide in temperate (50–64 °F) waters, and some also are found in tropical (over 64 °F) waters. They swim from the surface to 6,600 feet.

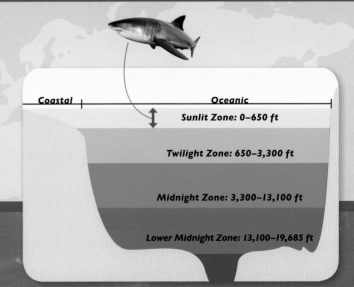

Coastal | Oceanic

Sunlit Zone: 0–650 ft

Twilight Zone: 650–3,300 ft

Midnight Zone: 3,300–13,100 ft

Lower Midnight Zone: 13,100–19,685 ft

SHARK ATTACKS

Whenever a shark attacks someone swimming offshore, it makes news all around the world, particularly if the victim is killed. But most experts agree that the risk of being attacked by a shark is very small.

Attacks are rare

Worldwide, there are only around 70 to 100 attacks in an average year, of which around 10 to 15 are fatal. More people are killed by bees each year than by sharks.

Surfing star

In October 2003, 13-year-old Bethany Hamilton was surfing off the coast of Hawaii when she was attacked by a tiger shark. It bit off her left arm. She survived the attack and returned to the water 26 days later. In 2007, she became a professional surfer.

hen sharks attack surfers, they
obably mistake the outline of
e surfboard for prey.

Survivor

One of world's leading
authorities on the great
white shark, Rodney Fox,
was himself the victim of
a terrible attack in 1963.
He was almost bitten
in half and his wounds
needed more than 450
stitches. Since then, he
has dedicated his life
to the appreciation and
preservation of the great
white shark.

fighting chance

nyone who is unlucky enough to be
tacked by a shark should try to fight
ack by hitting the shark on its snout
nd clawing at its eyes and gills.

e eyes and
out are a shark's
lnerable areas.

Great white shark
A great white breaks the surface of the water as it hunts for food. These are the largest predatory fish in the oceans. Their bite is about twice as powerful as that of a lion.

OCEANS IN DANGER

The oceans are important to people. We transport essential goods on them by ship and get food and natural resources from the sea. However, we also damage the oceans through pollution and overfishing, and this creates problems for sharks.

Sharks sometimes becom tangled in nets and die.

Dangers of pollution

When there is an oil spill or when waste materials are dumped at sea, humans are contributing to the pollution of the oceans. Pollution can contaminate fish that come into contact with it. When sharks eat contaminated fish, they end up with high levels of dangerous chemicals in their bodies.

Accidents at sea often lead to ocean pollution.

Polluting sewage

Millions of gallons of sewage are emptied into the oceans each year by people. Fish that live in coastal waters can be harmed by sewage. This also harms sharks that feed on the fish living in these waters.

DISCOVERY FACT™

Some tourist resorts put shark nets off the shoreline to keep sharks away from the beach. Sharks, turtles, dolphins, and rays can all get tangled and die in these nets.

Garbage dumped at sea

Waste material thrown into the sea includes discarded fishing lines, nets, and plastics in which sharks sometimes get entangled. If they cannot get free, they will die in the water.

Not many young

Sharks are slow to mature and may produce just a few young in any breeding cycle. This means that when populations are hit by overfishing or ocean pollution, the numbers take a very long time to recover.

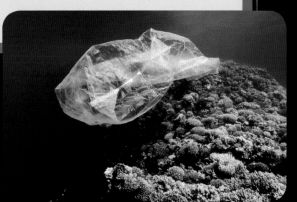

SHORTFIN MAKO SHARK

This is one of the fastest sharks in the ocean. It can reach speeds of up to 30 miles per hour when chasing after prey and can leap clear out of the water to heights of up to 20 feet.

The shortfin mako shark's upper side is metallic blue while the underside is white. This pattern is known as countershading. It makes the shark hard to spot in the water when seen both from above and from below.

The shortfin mako's speed allows it to feed on quick-moving fish, such as tuna, swordfish, and even other sharks. It is able to hunt them because it swims faster than they do.

Due to their size and speed, shortfin makos can be dangerous to humans. There have been a number of attacks on swimmers and divers, and some of them have been fatal. Divers have reported that the shark will swim in a figure-of-eight pattern before launching an attack with its mouth open.

Body shape
Sleek and streamlined with a long, cone-shaped snout. It slips easily through the water, which helps the shark to swim so fast.

Profile

Length:	Average 5.9–8.2 ft (males and females), 12.8 ft maximum
Weight:	Average 132–300 lb (males and females), 1,250 lb maximum
Order:	Mackerel sharks
Family:	Mackerel sharks
Diet:	Fish including other sharks, rays, squid, dolphins (right), small whales

Teeth
Slender, slightly curved, and pointed teeth, with razor-sharp edges, help the mako grip slippery, fast-moving fish.

Location
Shortfin mako sharks are found worldwide in warm temperate (16 to 64 °F) and tropical (over 64 °F) waters. They swim from the surface to around 500 feet.

Coastal — Oceanic

Sunlit Zone: 0–650 ft

Twilight Zone: 650–3,300 ft

Midnight Zone: 3,300–13,100 ft

Lower Midnight Zone: 13,100–19,685 ft

GLOBAL WARMING

Global warming is the gradual increase in temperature of the Earth's atmosphere. Scientists believe that this will cause climates to change, sea levels to rise, and extreme weather to become more common.

The oceans are important to our planet because they absorb carbon dioxide from the atmosphere. Sharks are a vital part of the marine habitat because they keep life in the oceans in healthy balance.

Changing habits

As the sea gets warmer, some marine animals change their behavior. They appear in places where they have not been seen before. Scientists believe that some time this century sharks will begin to be seen in the ocean around Antarctica.

Reefs in danger

Warming seas around coral reefs can cause devastation. The coral dies and turns white. This deprives reef fish of food and shelter, and their population drops. This, in turn, means that the reef sharks struggle to find food.

Polluting the atmosphere

Global warming is thought to be caused by an increase in greenhouse gases such as carbon dioxide. These gases trap heat in the atmosphere. Carbon dioxide is produced when oil, gas, and coal are burned.

What can we do?

Everybody can help to slow down global warming by walking and cycling because this does not burn oil. If we travel in airplanes, buses, or cars, carbon dioxide is produced, which may speed up global warming.

Beautiful natural habitats like this coral reef are threatened by rising sea temperatures.

PROTECTING SHARKS

Although changes in the world's weather, the effects of pollution, and the impact of fishing all spell danger for sharks, many people are trying to protect and conserve shark populations around the globe.

Shark sanctuaries

Some countries have banned commercial fishing in their national waters (the parts of the sea that they control), to help protect sharks. The island groups of Palau, in the western Pacific Ocean, and the Maldives, in the Indian Ocean, have both done this.

Palau, a country made up of around 250 Pacific islands, has created a protected area for sharks.

Acting responsibly

Tourists who want to see and swim with sharks should make sure that the dive company treats sharks with proper care.

How can we help?

We can help sharks survive in the wild by not buying shark products, which encourages shark fishing. We can also try to persuade politicians to change the laws that govern how commercial fishing is done. Some people are trying to get laws changed so that sharks are better protected.

Better understanding

Scientific research, sea life visitor centers, television programs, magazine articles, movies, and books all help the general public to understand that sharks are remarkable creatures.

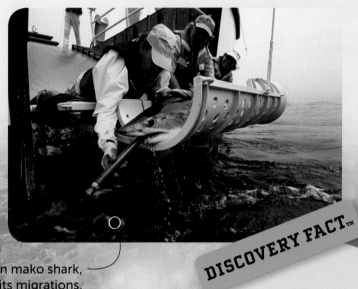

Scientists tag a shortfin mako shark, to help track its migrations.

Aquariums are great places to learn about sharks and see them close up.

DISCOVERY FACT™

Scientists in New Zealand have tagged a mako shark so that it can be tracked by satellite. It traveled more than 8,260 miles in 7 months, sometimes swimming more than 60 miles in a day.

Whale shark
A whale shark glides through the water surrounded by smaller fish and almost as many scuba divers.

GLOSSARY

Algae
Organisms that are mostly found in water and are generally very small.

Amphipod
A tiny, shrimplike crustacean that lives in the water.

Aquatic
Relating to water. Aquatic animals all live in water.

Baleen
Sievelike material in the mouths of some whales. Used to filter-feed.

Barbel
Whisker-like feelers near the nostrils and mouth of some sharks. Used to taste and feel.

Bioluminescence
The ability of a living organism to produce light.

Bivalve
A mollusk that has two shells that are hinged together.

Camouflage
A special coloring or body shape that blends with the surroundings, so that an animal is not easily seen by predators or prey.

Carnivore
An animal that eats other animals.

Cartilage
Tough, light, and stretchy material from which a shark's skeleton is made.

Colony
A group of animals living together.

Continental shelf
The seafloor that slopes gradually from a continent down to a depth of about 650 feet.

Copepod
A tiny, shrimplike crustacean that lives in the water.

Crustacean
An invertebrate animal that has an outer shell (an exoskeleton) and jointed legs, such as lobsters, crabs, and shrimps.

Diatom
A type of plant plankton with a hard, shell-like skeleton made of two halves.

Dorsal fin
The tall fin that stands upright on a shark's back.

Echinoderms
Marine animals that have arms or rays, such as starfish and sea urchins.

Equator
An imaginary line that runs around the Earth's surface, halfway between the two poles.

Frond
The leaflike part of a seaweed.

Gill
The parts of the body used by fish and some other animals to breathe underwater.

Gravity
The force that attracts objects toward large bodies, such as the Earth or Sun.

Habitat
The name given to the place where an animal or plant lives.

Invertebrate
An animal that does not have a backbone.

Kelp
Large seaweeds that grow in underwater forests in shallow seas.

Lagoon
An area of salty water cut off from the sea by a bank of shingle, sand, or coral.

Larva
The growing stage of an animal such as a young fish or squid.

Mammal
A warm-blooded animal. Female mammals give birth to live young and feed them with their own milk.

Marine
To do with the sea.

Microscopic
Too small to be seen with the naked eye.

Migration
A regular journey made by an animal, sometimes over very long distances.

Mollusk
An animal with a soft
body, usually protected
by an outer shell.

Mucus
A thick, slimy fluid that
an organism produces
to protect itself.

Nocturnal
Being active at night rather
than during the day.

Nutrient
A substance that is needed for
healthy growth and living.

Organism
A living thing such as an animal,
plant, fungus, or bacterium.

Parasite
An animal that lives off another
animal (the host) without doing
anything to benefit the host.

Pectoral fins
The fins that stick out of
the sides of a shark's body
just behind its gills.

Photosynthesis
The process by which plants
use sunlight and the green
chlorophyll in their leaves to make
sugars that give the plant energy.

Phytoplankton
Tiny plants that float freely
in the ocean currents.

Plankton
The tiny plants and animals that
are found floating close to the
surface of ponds, lakes, and seas.

Polar
To do with the areas around
the North and South Poles.

Pollution
The act of making something,
such as the air or the water,
unclean by discharging
harmful substances into it.

Population
The number of individuals
living in a particular area.

Predator
An animal that hunts and
feeds on other animals.

Prey
An animal that is hunted
by other animals.

Pupil
The central part of an
eye that lets in light.

Respiratory system
The parts of a body that allow
an organism to breathe.

Sensor
Part of an organism that responds
to a particular stimulus, such
as light, sound, or heat.

Shoal
A group of fish that
swim together.

Solitary
A plant or animal that lives alone.

Sonar
A way of finding the position
of objects or prey by using
sound waves that travel
through the water.

Streamlined
Having a shape that slips
easily through air or a liquid,
like a torpedo, for instance.

Structure
The way something is
built or put together.

Submersible
A vessel used for undersea
exploration. It can have a human
crew, or it can be unmanned.

Swim bladder
A gas-filled organ inside
a fish that stops it from
sinking in the water.

Tentacle
A long, feeler-like structure found
on certain animals, such as
jellyfish, anemones, and squid.

Tropical
Relating to a part of the Earth
that lies close to the equator. The
climate in the tropical zone is hot
and wet for most of the year.

Tsunami
A big wave created by
an earthquake occurring
under the ocean.

Vertebrate
An animal that has a backbone.

Zooplankton
Tiny animals that float freely
in the ocean currents.

INDEX

Picture Credits

a = above, b = below, l = left, r = right, c = center.

© **Shutterstock:** 12-13, 148-149; A Cotton Photo 132bl, 148b; Achimdiver 84b; Jim Agronick 8-9; Greg Amptman's Undersea Discoveries 24-25, 50-51, 54-55, 81a, 166-167, 170br, 184-185, 195b, 198-199, 206a; Andreas Altenburger 200b; aquapix 126-127; Egor Arkhipov 190cl; Mike Bauer 187cr; BioLife Pics 185a; Willyam Bradberry 1, 2-3, 30-31, 106-107, 160-161, 206-207, 213ar; Brandelet 22-23, 90-91; Tiago Sá Brito 190bl; Henner Damke 175b; DiDiver 162-163; digitalbalance 36a, 137a; Mark Doherty 196-197; Dray van Beeck 23ar, 130-131, 152-153; Sergey Dubrov 154-155; Rich Carey 26a, 105a, 108-109, 112b, 116-117, 152b, 155a, 214b; Cheryl Casey 210b; Catmando 91a, cbpix 20-21, 62b, 99b, 124-125, 140b; cdelacy 204-205; Nantawat Chotsuwan 77a; Chris von Damm 120-121; EpicStockMedia 156b; Dan Exton 113cr; FAUP 23br, 34-35, 36b, 42bl, 87b; prochasson frederic 174bl; jarvis gray 206b, Rui Manuel Teles Gomes 153cr; Shane Gross 170-171, 186-187; Agnieszka Guzowska 30bl; hainaultphoto 211br; hanzl 72-73; Elliotte Rusty Harold 197al; Tony Hunt 208-209; jaytee 153al; jefras 200-201; Gail Johnson 32-33; kataleewan intarachote 58-59; stephan kerkhofs 122-123; KKulikov 214-215; D. Kucharski K. Kucharska 186b; Liquid Productions, LLC 60b, 170cl; Susana_Martins 183b; Dudarev Mikhail 69, 216; mrfiza 187al; mrHanson 80-81; Andrey Myagkov 180-181 (background), 224; Narchuk 40-41; Stephen Nash 11cr; Natursports 156-157; Amanda Nicholls 170bl; nicolas.voisin44 18-19; Krzysztof Odziomek 136-137, 147cr; optionm 216ar; Boris Pamikov 138b, 188-189; Sergey Popov V 112a; Real Deal Photo 139ar; Michael Rosskothen 28-29, Ian Scott 6-7, 98a, 104-105, 118-119, 129a, 150-151; Anna segeren 97al; serrnovik 190-191; solarseven 220-221, 222-223, Stubblefield Photography 144-145, 189br; Kuttelvaserova Stuchelova 73br;

Teguh Tirtaputra 172b; tororo reaction 202b; Mogens Trolle 203b; tubuceo 92-93; Vilainecrevette 135ar, 138-139; Vlad61 94-95; Joanne Weston 134-135; Richard Whitcombe 211bl; Wong Hock weng 44b; yize 201br; Zeamonkey Images 218-219.

© **Dreamstime.com:** 37b, 46cl, 75bc, 78b, 79a, 103l, 110a, 122br, 140-141; John Abramo 96cr; Wolfgang Amri 27a; John Anderson 97r; Lucila De Avila 31cr; Darren Baker 132-133; Bernard Beton 68bl; Mikhail Blajenov 114-115a; Harald Bolten 64b; Wei Send Chen 118b; Chinieh 94b; Dragan Cvetanovic 200ac; Tom Davison 215al; Cathy Figuli 45ar; Fotograf77 85a; Franky 123ar; Igor Groshev 48br; Simon Gurney 43r, 53a; Inga Ivanova 144b; Olga Khoroshunova 122bl; Kwerry 128a; Andrea Leone 45b, 113a; David Lloyd 84-85; Dirk-jan Mattaar 111bl; memm74 127al; Cornelis Opstal 129r; Nick Poling 53b; Radu Razvan 73ar; Laurin Rinder 46cr; Chris Ryan 75ar; Dejan Sarman 80b; Matthew Scholey 38-39; Tommy Schultz 141a; Ian Scott 44-45a; Asther Lau Choon Siew 96b, 106a, 106b, 128b, 144ar, 145b, 183a; Miguel Angelo Silva 47br; Beverly Speed 118a; John Stublar 49a; Jeff Waibel 74l; Matthias Weinrich 26-27; Jan Martin Will 48cl; Holger Wulschlaeger 103r.

© **Getty Images:** Robert Arnold 46bl; Auscape / UIG 72b; Mark Conlin 191a, 217a; Peter David 179b; Karen Doody / Stocktrek Images 157b; Dorling Kindersley 173al; P. Ginet-Drin / Photocuisine 21bl; Image Source 4-5, 216-217; Wayne Lynch 52ar, 202-203; Zac Macaulay 78-79bc; Terry Moore / Stocktrek Images 88-89; Louise Murray 66-67; National Geographic 15cr, 182a; Oxford Scientific 11b, 70-71; Doug Perrine 165b, 181b; Wolfgang Poelzer 135r; Jeff Rotman 168-169, 207a, 210-211; Brian J. Skerry 158-159; Masa Ushioda 212-213; Gary Vestal 74c; Visuals Unlimited, Inc. / Andy Murch 76-77, 82-83; Visuals Unlimited, Inc. / Louise Murray 164-165; Visuals

Unlimited, Inc. / Michael Ready 178a; Stuart Westmorland 146-147.

© **Corbis:** Theo Allofs 86a; Tony Arruza 133cr; Bettmann 200ac; Brandon D Cole 65ar, 113bl, 189bl; Tim Davis 6-7, 12ar; DK Limited 84ac; Stephen Frink 20br, 52b; Carson Ganci / Design Pics 16-17; Bob Gomel 148a; Klaas Lingbeek-van Kranen 64-65; Amos Nachoum 13ar, 20bl; New Zealand Ministry of Fisheries / epa 180b; Rick Price 174-175; Louie Psihoyos 17bl; Jeffrey L. Rotman 11ar, 15a, 22ac, 74-75, 80a, 107br; Denis Scott 12-13, 14-15, 21br; Sea Life Park / Reuters 176-177; Harish Tyagi / epa 39b; Visuals Unlimited 180-181c; Stuart Westmorland 195a; Ralph White 56b, 57a; Douglas P. Wilson / Frank Lane Picture Agency 11al, 22bl.

© **istockphoto.com:** 63a, 78a, 86b, 91b, 107a, 111r, 126bl, 129cl, 161bl, 215br, Charles Babbitt 173b; Lim Weng Chai 201ac; Chris Dascher 99a; RbbrDckyBK 122a; David Safanda 140ar; Dan Schmitt 114b, 119b; Adam Schneider 110b; Kristian Sekulic 161cr; Luis Carlos Torres 149b; Adam White 87a.

NOAA (National Oceanic and Atmospheric Administration): 39b, 57br, 63b, 64a, 68cr, 96ar, 98bl, 127br 166ar, 173a, 174c, 178cl, 180ar, 182b, 188bl, 194cr, 194b, 196ac, 196bl, 196br.

© **NASA (National Aeronautic and Space Administration):** 38b, 61r, 102cr.

© **USGS (United States Geological Survey):** 183cr.

© **Digital Vision:** 22cr, 43tl.

© **Creative Commons:** 68al; Citron 192-193.

© David Burdick 115br; Chris & Monique Fallows / OceanwideImages.com 46-47; Peter Herring / imagequestmarine com 167al; Uwe Kils 62ac, 164c; Peter Parks / imagequestmarine.com 178br, Douglas P. Wilson 61bl.